CONTENTS

ACKNOWLEDGEMENTS

This study was funded by the Department of Education and Science. We are particularly indebted to the comments and suggestions of Breda Naughton, Mary Dunne, Cearbhall Ó Dálaigh and Muiris O'Connor.

We wish to make a special note of thanks to the six schools who participated in the case studies. We are grateful to the school principals who gave so generously of their time and to the Junior and Leaving Certificate students who completed the questionnaires.

Within the ESRI, we acknowledge the unfailing support of the Director, Brendan Whelan, and the valuable comments of Helen Russell, Philip J. O'Connell and Edgar Morgenroth. The staff of the survey unit were, as always, professional and diligent in their work. We are especially grateful to James Williams (Head of the Survey Unit). Finally, Pat Hopkins is to be thanked for her efficient production of copies of the versions of the report.

LIST OF TABLES

AT WORK IN SCHOOL

Part-Time Employment among Second-Level Students

Selina McCoy and *Emer Smyth*

The Liffey Press
in association with
The Economic and Social Research Institute

Published by
The Liffey Press
Ashbrook House
10 Main Street
Raheny, Dublin 5, Ireland
www.theliffeypress.com

© 2004 The Economic and Social Research Institute

A catalogue record of this book is
available from the British Library.

ISBN 1-904148-54-9

Printed in Spain by Graficas Cems.

LIST OF FIGURES

Chapter One

INTRODUCTION

1.1: INTRODUCTION/CONTEXT OF THE STUDY

In the Irish context, little is known about the kinds of students who have a paid job while at school or about the impact of their job on their academic career. There is a generally held belief that levels of employment among students have risen over time and schools and teachers have been to the fore in expressing concerns over the effects of (rising) employment on students' school participation and attainments. A recent study (Morgan, 2000) carried out in sixteen Dublin schools found that three-quarters of Junior Cert, fifth year and Leaving Cert students held a part-time job. However, this study was unable to assess the impact of part-time work on exam performance or other student outcomes. The present study sets out to address this knowledge gap and seeks to examine comprehensively the extent of student employment, the objective and subjective characteristics of workers and non-workers, the nature of the jobs in which students engage and the effects of that employment on a range of academic and social outcomes.

Before examining the current state of Irish and international research in this area and setting out the key questions this study attempts to address, it seems important to set the study in the context of the labour market and economic climate within which young people seek work and the legislation governing their participation in such employment. In addition, the trends in educational participation and retention over recent decades are also considered, particularly as they relate to the changing composition of students remaining in school to Leaving Cert level and the extent of financial need among students.

The prevalence of working while at school must be seen in the context of overall changes in employment levels in Ireland since the early 1990s. Total employment grew by 26,400 per annum between 1990 and 1995 and by 76,400 per annum between 1995 and 2000 (Sexton, 2002). Growth was particularly dramatic in the market services sector, that is, in the sector which has more "casual" and part-time jobs which suit students. The extent to which this shift in employment drew young people into the labour market is evident among third-level students whose labour force participation increased from 7 per cent in 1991 to 40 per cent in 1999 (McCoy et al., 2000). However, lack of available data means it is harder to document the impact of employment availability on second-level students.

Regarding the legislative context, two recent pieces of legislation impose certain limitations on the employment of young people. Firstly, the *Protection of Young Persons (Employment) Act, 1996* and secondly, a code of practice *Concerning the Employment of Young Persons in Licensed Premises* published in July 2001.

The 1996 Act replaces the *Protection of Young Persons (Employment) Act, 1977* and considerably tightens the restrictions on the employment of young people. It indicates that a student must be at least 15 years of age to be employed during the school term (exemptions are made for the employment of 14- and 15-year-olds as part of an approved work experience or educational programme). During term-time the maximum working week for 15-year-olds is eight hours and under-16s may not be required to work before 8.00 am or after 8.00 pm. Students aged 16 and 17 years may work up to 10.00 pm at night and, during term-time, to 11.00 pm on weekend nights where there is no school the next day. The maximum working day for 16- and 17-year-olds is eight hours but no legal maximum term-time working week is specified. Before employing a young person an employer must see evidence of age and, before employing under-16s, must get written permission of a parent. The full provisions of the Act do not apply to the employment of close relatives and employment in fishing, shipping or the defence forces.

The 2001 Code of Practice arose from collaboration between a number of unions and associations representing employers in the hotel/restaurant and vintners trade and parents. It contains two important requirements, relating to the employment of second-level students:

1. *Study time*: "Provision should be made for students with impending examinations. These should allow for study leave and leave to sit exams, without having to work excessive hours in the period approaching the exams. Employers shall ensure that a student's job is protected in the event of his/her returning to work following study/exam leave."

2. *Parental permission*: written permission of the parents/guardian must be obtained.

As the Skills Initiative Unit (2002) observes, however, the code fails to make any reference to a maximum working week during term-time. It alludes to "excessive hours" without defining it and likewise with regard to the "pre-examination period". Study leave is advocated prior to examinations but the year-long requirement for students to complete regular homework is not mentioned. Finally, the document refers to "examinations" but it is unclear whether these include school term and annual examinations or relate solely to state examinations, that is, the Junior and Leaving Certificate examinations.

Serious questions remain, however, regarding the enforcement of the legislation relating to young people participating in paid employment. Comments by the Minister of State for Youth Affairs, Mr Willie O'Dea (*Irish Times*, 11 January 2001), suggest that legislation in this area is more often breached than observed and it has been argued that the number of inspectors would need to be at least doubled to 34 to ensure the effective enforcement of the Act. In total, six employers were convicted in 2000 in respect of breaches under this legislation, while over 2,700 inspections were carried out over the period January 2000 to July 2001 (Department of Enterprise, Trade and Employment, 24 July 2001).

Finally, the incidence of part-time employment must be considered in the context of the proportions of students persisting in second-level schooling and consequently the composition of the student body. A dramatic increase in participation at both secondary and tertiary levels in Ireland has been evident since the early 1980s. Between 1980 and 1998, the proportion of students taking the Leaving Certificate exam increased from 60 to 82 per cent. However, in spite of much higher levels of participation, participation rates continue to be strongly influenced by socio-economic background with much higher participation among those from professional backgrounds than among those from unskilled manual backgrounds (see Figure 1.1). The trend has been one of *absolute* growth in participation levels for all social groups but the *relative* pattern of inequality has remained remarkably unchanged (see Smyth and Hannan, 2000; Smyth, 1999). Such absolute growth in levels of participation in second level raises questions regarding the need for certain groups of students to enter the labour market while still at school and whether such need has grown as a result of expanding participation.

Figure 1.1: Leaving Certificate completion over time

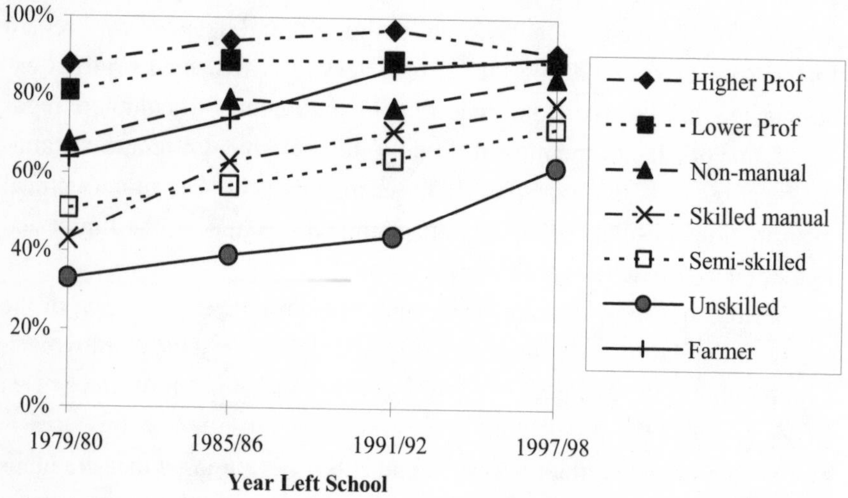

Source: ESRI Annual School Leavers' Survey, various years.

In sum, a number of contradictory trends have shaped the context within which young people in Ireland decide whether or not to take up paid employment while at school. On the one hand, the growth of employment, particularly in the services sector, has increased the accessibility of part-time work for young people. On the other hand, there have been legislative attempts at curtailing the employment of school-age children, particularly those in the younger age groups. Finally, there has been a considerable expansion in educational participation and retention, with the vast majority of young people now persisting in school to Leaving Cert level. This raises issues of the financial need to engage in part-time employment, particularly among those who had previously terminated their education and entered the labour market at a much earlier stage. The remainder of the study is concerned with exploring how these factors have prevailed in shaping the incidence and nature of part-time work among second-level students.

1.2: EXISTING RESEARCH ON PART-TIME EMPLOYMENT AMONG STUDENTS

1.2.1: Introduction

This review considers studies of student employment from a range of countries, principally because of the dearth of research emanating from the Irish context. However, it should be noted that youth employment will reflect the particular economic, social, cultural and institutional context within which it is located. As a result, findings regarding part-time employment among students in other countries may not necessarily be applicable to the Irish context. In the United States, for example, the practice of second-level (high school) students working to support car ownership is widespread and generally accepted. However, patterns of car ownership are different in the Irish context and this may partially influence the number and kinds of students who take on paid employment. Because of the focus of this study, the review focuses mainly on studies of second-level students, although some reference is made to employment among those within higher education.

Much of the literature distinguishes between two conflicting effects of engaging in part-time work while pursuing full-time education. The first argument, variously termed the time allocation effect or the zero-sum model, posits that work simply consumes time, competes with other activities such as education and displaces any alternative activities. As such, students who engage in employment will have less time and energy to devote to educational pursuits. Conversely, the second argument holds that early labour market experience can have positive socialisation or developmental effects: such work can promote the learning of new habits or attitudes, it can give early work experience, it can promote time-management among students, it can provide opportunities to interact in an adult rather than peer-based environment, it can promote responsibility, it can increase self-esteem and can enable the learning of new and valuable skills. The research literature is highly divided as to which of the arguments prevails: studies exist to support both sides, with no overall consensus as to the implications of part-time employment for subsequent educational, social and career outcomes.

1.2.2: Prevalence of employment among second-level students

Research in the US context has indicated that the level and intensity of student employment is responsive to the economic cycle in general and to local labour market demand in particular (Ruhm, 1997), with students working longer hours as local labour market demand increases (Ahituv and Tienda, 2000). This would suggest that, in the context of overall employment growth, part-time employment among second-level students in Ireland is likely to have increased. However, there has been little systematic research in the Irish context on this issue.

Evidence from the British context indicates rising participation in part-time employment by full-time students in the UK over a twenty-four year period (Micklewright et al., 1994). The authors relate this increase to the growth in the services sector, particularly in demand for part-time and casual workers. In addition, they maintain that rising retention rates have led to an increase in the proportion of teenagers from poorer families who need to work to support themselves financially.

There have been two studies in Northern Ireland examining the incidence of employment among full-time students. Leonard (1995) looks at part-time employment among undergraduates in Queen's University Belfast and finds 46 per cent in part-time employment. McVicar and McKee (2001), using the 1999 sweep of the Status Zero Survey in Northern Ireland, report an employment rate of 35 per cent among students in post-compulsory education. They argue that this lower figure (relative to international standards) may derive from fewer employment opportunities in Northern Ireland and the fact that students may be discouraged from taking up jobs by the relatively low wages on offer.[1]

---

[1] The survey pre-dated the introduction of the minimum wage into Northern Ireland.

Finally, and most recently, Morgan (2000) examines the prevalence of part-time employment among students in 16 Dublin schools, half of which are designated disadvantaged. He finds high levels of employment among Junior Cert, fifth year and Leaving Cert students with approximately three-quarters working outside school hours. There was little difference between boys and girls in levels of employment, and no notable variation was evident between students in disadvantaged schools and other students in their employment patterns.

1.2.3: "Quality" of student jobs

Evidence from the British context indicates the concentration of student workers in service occupations, particularly sales jobs. A similar pattern was found among students in Dublin schools (Morgan, 2000). A number of studies have emphasised the relatively poor quality of student jobs in terms of enhancing the "human capital" of young people. Greenberger and Steinberg (1986) suggest that youth jobs entail few chances to work co-operatively and involve little formal or informal training. Furthermore, some authors have suggested a change over time in the characteristics of jobs held by students, with a general decline in job quality and proportionately fewer students working in jobs which promote skill development (Stern et al, 1990, quoted in Schoenhals, Tienda and Schneider, 1998).

1.2.4: "Effects" of part-time employment

Numerous studies have indicated the positive effects of part-time work. According to a study by Carr, Wright and Brody (1996), working is found to have a positive effect on a variety of labour force outcomes, including labour force participation, employment status and income, even a decade after leaving school. Similarly, Ruhm (1997) finds an overall positive labour market benefit to working part-time, with student workers going on to earn higher wages and enter higher status jobs. Robinson (1999), in the Australian context, found that working longer hours while at school was associated with reduced post-school unemployment and, for some students, with higher wages. The positive effects of part-time work persist after controlling for the kinds of students who work part-time and are robust across a variety of specifications, samples and estimation techniques. Essentially, it appears that engaging in part-time work enables contact with potential future employers and it may also allow employers to screen possible future employees.

In addition, some studies have highlighted the positive effect of part-time work on the educational career itself. Oettinger (1999) argues that employment may increase the productivity of study time if it complements academic effects, for example, by increasing motivation or "future-orientedness". In addition, the option of part-time work may mean that those who need a current income may be more inclined to stay in full-time education than if faced with a choice between working full-time or not at all (Micklewright et al., 1994). As D'Amico (1984) argues:

> The enforced and prolonged dependency engendered by education can be counteracted with work involvement, which provides opportunities to assume greater responsibility, authority, and co-operative interdependence . . . employment experiences can then be viewed as preparatory socialisation that eases the psychological and social trauma associated with the often unsettling school-to-work transition (p. 153).

Furthermore, early work experience may strengthen the intentions of students to remain in school if they are engaged in jobs which are monotonous, poorly paid and physically demanding.

However, a good deal of research has been concerned with the possibility that positive labour market outcomes may be achieved at the cost of educational attainment and progression. Some studies have found no relationship between part-time work per se and educational attainment. D'Amico (1984), for example, finds no average effect of working on academic achievement. Similarly, Gade and Peterson (1980) find no significant effects of employment on academic achievement and self-esteem. However, a number of other studies have highlighted the negative impact of part-time work, especially of high levels of employment intensity (that is, longer hours) on educational outcomes.

Some studies report a negative linear relationship between hours worked and academic outcomes. Marsh (1991), for example, found that total hours worked unfavourably affected (in order of size) going to college, high school attendance, academic track, parental involvement, educational aspirations, standardised test scores and academic self-concept. These negative effects were a linear function of the number of hours worked and were consistent across sex, ability and socio-economic status groups. Research from a number of different national contexts has indicated a threshold below which the effects of part-time employment are positive (or at worst, neutral) and above which part-time work has a negative effect. Different studies have indicated different thresholds, varying from 10 to 20 hours. In the US context, D'Amico (1984) found that more intensive work involvement was associated with reduced study time while less intensive work involvement was found to have almost no effect (see also Lillydahl, 1990). Similarly, Post and Pong (2000), in analysing the US National Educational Longitudinal Survey data find positive effects on achievement when students are working up to 10 hours per week, non-significant effects for 11 to 20 hours and negative effects over 20 hours. Oettinger (1999) finds that intensive involvement in school year employment has a negative effect on grade point average. Similarly, Ruhm (1997) concludes that employment reduces educational attainment, particularly where that employment is in excess of 20 hours per week.

Robinson (1999) indicated that, in the Australian context, working longer hours was associated with lower completion rates in secondary school and lower grades. In the UK, Payne (2001) found that working more than 15 hours in Year 12 and more than 10 hours in Year 13 were negatively related to A-level results. Similarly, Singh (1998) using longitudinal data, finds that the number of hours worked had a significant negative effects on retention, standardised achievement and achievement in particular subject areas, controlling for earlier achievement and background characteristics. However, Singh does not interpret this pattern as a wholly harmful phenomenon, arguing that early immersion into the labour market may enhance choice and control among students who are weakly engaged in school life or dissatisfied, rather than their being constrained to remain in an institution they dislike.

It is also important to explore whether the effects of part-time employment vary by the type of job and by gender, age group, educational stage, and educational track. According to McNeal (1997), jobs can be classified according to the degree of structure imposed, the amount and type of supervision received, the level of skills and/or training required, the use of higher order thinking skills and whether the job setting is peer or adult based. While babysitting, for example, allows a degree of flexibility and choice on the part of the student, more formal jobs such as those in the retail sector are more structured and less flexible. Similarly, Markel and Frone (1998) take account of three aspects of employment — job hours, job dissatisfaction and workload — and examine the impact on three outcomes — school readiness, school performance and school dissatisfaction. They argue for the need to examine the quality of employment, not simply the number of hours worked. They find that those who work longer hours and are exposed to undesirable work environments are more likely to experience work-school conflict, which in turn may lead to poor academic outcomes. They recommend that intervention efforts should focus on the workplace; work-schedule flexibility and job enrichment should be implemented to maximise the positive outcomes of student employment. There is also some evidence (Marsh, 1991) to suggest that the effects may vary depending on young people's motivations for working. This study found that students who worked to save money for college had favourable effects on the majority (15 of the 22) of the outcomes examined.

1.2.5: Gender and class variation in employment prevalence and effects

In the Northern Irish context, McVicar and McKee (2001) find evidence that academically able young people are over-represented among part-time workers as are female students. Higher social class youth are more likely to work and those with unemployed fathers are less likely to work, a pattern which they argue reflects employability, local labour demand and family networking factors. Schill et al. (1985) also find that middle-class students are more likely to have a job, although they tend to work fewer hours than their lower socio-economic counterparts. They refute the argument that young people work because of economic need, finding a curvilinear relationship between socio-economic status and labour force participation or hours worked. Interestingly, they also find a positive relationship between mother's employment and student's employment. Similarly, Dustmann, Rajah and Smith (1997) find that adverse family circumstances (such as parental unemployment) has no significant impact on the likelihood of engaging in part-time employment while at school. Furthermore, Oettinger (1999) finds that students of high ability are disproportionately likely to hold regular jobs with low hour requirements.

There is some evidence that the effects of part-time employment vary between different groups of students. Ruhm (1997) finds the negative impact of heavy work commitments is much greater for females with forty hours of employment being predicted to reduce completed years of schooling almost five times as much for women as for men. Conversely, Ahituv and Tienda (2000) report that women who have some attachment to the labour market are less likely to withdraw from school, but high work intensity does, however, significantly increase the likelihood of withdrawal for women. In drawing on cross-national TIMSS (Third International Maths and Science Study) data, Post and Pong (2000) find that across most countries the effects of part-time work on Maths and Science achievement are more detrimental for boys than for girls. However, they note that these differences could relate to the degree of stigma attached to work (particularly for girls), gender differences in the number of hours worked and in the type of work being done with jobs being performed by girls perhaps less likely to interfere with school.

1.2.6: Selection effect?

One possible reason for the apparent inconsistency in research findings in this area may relate to the possible selection effects operating. While some studies attempt to model this possible selection bias, others do not. McNeal (1997), for example, argues that:

1. Students who are more inclined to drop out to begin with select themselves into the workforce and into the worst jobs with more hours of work;

2. Students who drop out are not more engaged in the work culture, but are less involved in schooling;

3. Students who select themselves into work hold different attitudes and orientations towards school than those who do not work.

Studies have utilised two main ways of attempting to address this issue. The first utilises longitudinal data to take account of factors affecting the likelihood of entering employment and then controlling for these factors in modelling the effects of employment on various outcomes. The second method draws on various statistical methodologies in attempting to statistically model differential propensities to engage in employment and how that might affect educational and other outcomes.

Longitudinal data have considerable advantages in studying the effects of part-time employment on student outcomes in that they allow researchers to identify the characteristics of working students at a point before they become involved in paid employment. Schoenhals, Tienda and Schneider (1998) attempt to address the issue of causality using a school detachment measure from an earlier time point (two years earlier). They find that students previously detached from school are more likely to work. In addition, they argue that much of the adverse effect of work on academic outcomes is attributable to pre-existing differences between young people who work at different intensities. Taking account of these selection effects, they contend that the effects of employment are much more modest and indirect than shown by earlier studies.

Singh (1998), using longitudinal data, finds that students with high prior achievement were less likely to work longer hours, while students with low previous achievement were more likely to work longer hours. Similarly, Steinberg, Fegley and Dornbusch (1993), drawing on longitudinal data, contend that the negative factors associated with student employment actually precede rather than result from working; students who work do not suffer academically compared to those who do not (with the exception of those who work 20 hours per week or more).

Longitudinal data are not available in many contexts, however. As a result, researchers have focused on developing statistical methods to control for differences between working and non-working students in looking at the effects on a range of outcomes. Hotz et al. (1999) focus on the robustness of previous attempts to control for unobserved heterogeneity and selectivity, that is, for the differences between the groups of workers and non-workers. They conclude that the estimated returns to working while in school are dramatically diminished in magnitude and significance when using these dynamic selection methods. McVicar and McKee (2001) use a "bivariate semi-ordered probit model". This approach entails developing two sets of models, the first exploring the factors influencing the decision to work and the second analysing the factors influencing exam performance; the two models are first estimated separately and then jointly. Using these estimation procedures, their results indicate that having a part-time job does not significantly affect qualification levels. However, when hours worked is taken into account, the authors find that working more than 15 hours per week has a negative effect on exam performance.

1.3: RESEARCH QUESTIONS

This study sets out to address the gap in research on the impact of part-time work on student outcomes in the Irish context. The main research questions are as follows:

1. What are the characteristics of those engaged in part-time employment during their second-level education?

2. Does participation in employment have a negative effect on school completion and examination performance?

3. Are any negative effects of part-time work due to the intensity of employment rather than part-time work per se?

4. Does work experience obtained while at school have a positive impact in helping students to make a smoother transition into the labour market?

The study sets out to inform the policy debate about part-time employment. In particular, it seeks to highlight the appropriate target for policy intervention. Should efforts be directed at the workplace attempting to promote enriching employment experiences for young people, minimising the hours of work, and/or ensuring adequate training and wages? Should interventions be targeted at schools to help them initiate school policies on student work? Should parents be made aware of the potentially damaging effects of certain types of work and excessive employment? Or should policy be focused on young people themselves, in attempting to strengthen their attachment to and satisfaction with school, in creating an understanding of the potentially negative impact of (excessive) employment or enabling them to manage multiple demands more effectively?

1.4: METHOLODOGY

The study used three complementary data sources in assessing the prevalence, nature and impact of part-time employment in the Irish context:

- The Annual School Leavers' Surveys conducted in 1999 and 2002;

- Data developed from a survey of schools conducted in 1994 for the *Coeducation and Gender Equality* project, subsequently developed for the *Do Schools Differ?* and *Who Chooses Science?* projects (hereafter termed the "Schools Database");

- A survey of students in six second-level schools carried out in late 2001.

Each Annual School Leavers' Survey is based on a national stratified sample of school leavers who are interviewed one year after leaving school. Thus the reference cohort for the 1999 survey year refers to those who left the official second-level system in the 1997/98 academic year (i.e. between September 1997 and the end of August 1998). The survey gathers a wealth of information about young people's social background, their educational attainment and performance, their post-school pathways and their early labour market experience. In addition, in 1999 valuable information was collected on young people's experience of part-time work while at school: including data on whether they worked, the school years during which they worked, along with the days and hours worked. These data are primarily used to examine the relationship between part-time work while at school and post-school labour market experiences.

The Schools Database collected information on the attitudes, aspirations and characteristics of almost 6,000 Junior Cert and 4,000 Leaving Cert students in 116 second-level schools across the country. The survey collected information on whether the student held a paid part-time job at the time of the survey (generally, February or March of their exam year) and on the number of hours usually worked. The survey data were supplemented by information on the examination performance of students.

For the Junior Cert cohort, data were subsequently obtained on whether the student had taken their Leaving Cert exam and the grades they received. The detailed information available about students allows us to control for a range of factors in assessing the potential impact of part-time work on school drop-out and examination performance.

Analyses of the Schools Database were used to highlight regional, social class, gender and school type variations in part-time work prevalence and allowed the identification of six schools representing these dimensions of variation. Table 1.1 below illustrates the characteristics of the six schools across these dimensions: a wide variety of school types and characteristics is represented among the six schools. Schools were primarily selected to capture variations in levels of part-time employment at the time of the 1994 survey. However, the schools represent a range of school types, including boys' and girls' secondary, community/comprehensive and vocational schools, and a variety of student profiles in terms of socio-economic background. In addition, a variety of school sizes, regional spread and urban/rural location are captured.

The adoption of a case study approach allowed for the in-depth study of students' experiences of part-time work. While not nationally representative, the administration of detailed questionnaires with all Junior and Leaving Cert students in the six schools allowed for a thorough exploration of students' experiences, motivations and decisions regarding part-time employment.

Within these schools, over 1,000 Junior Cert and Leaving Cert students completed questionnaires in November/December 2001 regarding their experiences of, and attitudes to, part-time work. Among the issues explored are students' perceptions of the impact of paid work on school work, exams, social life and skills acquisition; students' perceptions of school life, their academic self-image and expectations; students' reasons for working and not working; and the expenditure patterns of student workers. These data allow us to explore students' own views on balancing study and paid work. In addition, interviews were conducted with principals in the six schools, providing an interesting insight into their perceptions regarding the prevalence and effects of student employment.

Table 1.1: Overview of Six Selected Schools, 2001 Survey

Sch	Region	Urban/ Rural	Size	School Type	Social Class Mix	Part-time Work Rate, 1994	N in Survey	Transition Year Provided
1	East	Urban	Large	Boys' Sec	Middle-class	Average	177	Yes
2	Mid-West	Large town	V large	Girls' Sec	Middle-class	Average	319	No
3	Midlands	Rural	Large	Comm/comp	Mixed	High	168	Yes
4	East	Urban	Medium	Vocational	Mixed	High	149	No
5	North-East	Town	Small	Vocational	Mixed/Working-Class	High	101	Yes
6	West	Rural	Small	Vocational	Mixed	Low	101	Yes

1.5: STRUCTURE OF THE REPORT

Chapter Two considers the prevalence of part-time employment among second-level students and how this has changed over time. It also examines the characteristics of workers and non-workers: both objective social background characteristics and subjective attitudinal characteristics are examined. The motivations behind part-time employment decisions are analysed in Chapter Three. Students' perceptions of their parents' and schools' views on part-time work are considered. In addition, the expenditure patterns of workers are examined. Chapter Four investigates the quality of jobs in which students engage, including the hours and days worked, the regularity of the work, the employment sector and earnings. The relationship between part-time employment and a range of student outcomes is analysed in Chapter Five. Among the outcomes studied are school dropout, examination performance, out-of-school activities and post-school transitions. Finally, Chapter Six summarises the key findings and looks at some of the implications for policy.

Chapter Two

PREVALENCE AND CHARACTERISTICS OF PART-TIME WORKERS

2.1: INTRODUCTION

Drawing on the three data sources detailed in Chapter 1, this chapter examines a number of aspects of school leavers' engagement in part-time work while at school. In particular, the chapter considers the incidence and prevalence of part-time work among second-level students, drawing mainly on the 1994 national survey and 1999 and 2002 Annual School Leavers' Surveys. Secondly, the characteristics of workers and non-workers are explored; both objective social background characteristics and subjective attitudinal characteristics are examined. Finally, the relationship between participation in part-time work and school type and curricular track is considered at a descriptive level.

2.1.1: Definition of Work

Part-time employment refers to any part-time job outside of school hours and not related to study or a course a student is taking. Students are asked to include any work done for pay, no matter how irregular it might be, including work which is not strictly speaking on the open labour market, such as "babysitting".[1] Where possible, we separate out the more informal and flexible babysitting-type jobs, given that they may have a different relationship to academic activities and examination performance. We also

---

[1] There are some variations between the data sources in the phrasing of the question regarding participation in part-time work: the 2001 survey explicitly states that engagement in babysitting-type employment is to be included as having a job, while no such reference is included in the School Leavers' Survey questionnaire.

attempt to differentiate, where possible, between regular weekly employment and employment which is of a less regular or less frequent nature.

2.2: PARTICIPATION IN PART-TIME WORK AMONG SECOND-LEVEL STUDENTS

2.2.1: Prevalence of part-time working

At the time of the 1994 national study, overall employment levels stood at a quarter of Junior Cert and 31 per cent of Leaving Cert students. Examining students in the six schools surveyed in 2001, 30 per cent of the Junior Certificate students and 37 per cent of the Leaving Certificate students in these schools had a job at the time of the 1994 survey.[2] By the time of the 2001 survey, however, 70 per cent of Junior Certificate students and 73 per cent of Leaving Certificate students in *these* six schools held a part-time job (Figure 2.1). Excluding those who cited babysitting as their main job (which may differ from other jobs in its flexibility, amount of hours involved and so on), 36 per cent of Junior Certificate students and 57 per cent of Leaving Certificate students held a part-time job in 2001. These figures suggest rising levels of part-time employment over the period.

Figure 2.1: Percentage working part-time: 1994 and 2001 Junior and Leaving Cert students

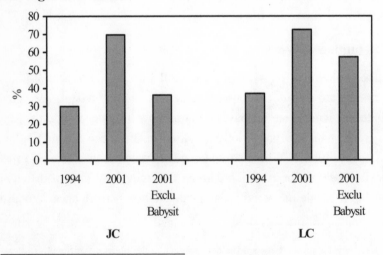

---

[2] The schools selected for the 2001 survey, therefore, slightly over-estimate the level of employment.

The six schools included in the 2001 survey varied in their levels of participation in part-time work (see Figures 2.2a and 2.2b). As discussed in Chapter 1, the schools vary in their location, type and composition.

Figure 2.2a: Percentage working part-time in Leaving Cert by school (1994 and 2001)

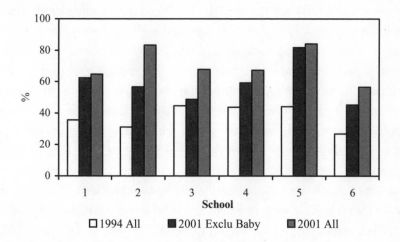

Figure 2.2b: Percentage Junior and Leaving Cert students working part-time (excluding babysitting) by school (2001)

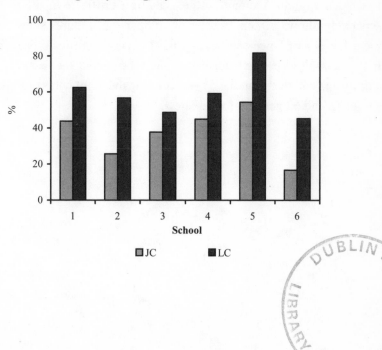

Examining the prevalence rates in Figures 2.2a and 2.2b (excluding babysitting-type jobs), the results show wide variation across the six schools in rates of work, patterns which still largely reflect those found in 1994. To illustrate, while 45 per cent of Leaving Certificate students in school 6 are engaged in part-time work (of a non-babysitting type), the corresponding level of employment in school 5 is over 80 per cent. The highest rates of work are found in three schools representing rural, urban and town locations, in midland, eastern and north-eastern regions. These schools were mixed in their socio-economic composition. The lowest levels of part-time employment are found in a rural school in the west, perhaps because of the more limited availability and accessibility of paid work in this region. Overall, the figures illustrate the variations in young people's propensity to work: variations which may reflect opportunity and accessibility of part-time work, school policy and practice, parental support and financial need. Essentially variations in work prevalence across the schools are not necessarily related to school differences per se but are also related to student intake and local labour market conditions.

Results from the Annual School Leavers' Surveys for 1999 and 2002 show evidence of rising part-time work levels over time (rising from 48 to 58 per cent, see Figure 2.3). However, the intensity of employment has fallen slightly. Examining the Leaving Certificate qualified leavers separately allows a more consistent comparison. Figures show employment levels of 61 per cent among the Leaving Certificate qualified cohort in 2002 (59 per cent for males and 62 per cent for females), a rate significantly higher than the 51 per cent for the 1999 cohort (50 per cent for males and 52 per cent for females).

Figure 2.3: Paid employment among Leaving Cert qualified leavers

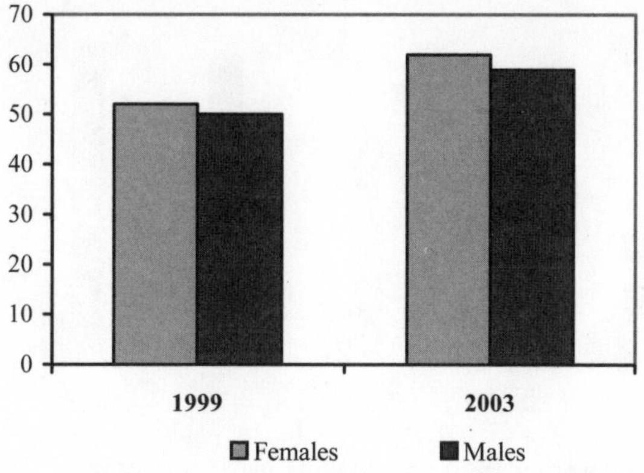

Source: School Leavers' Surveys, 1999 and 2002.

A further source of information on levels of part-time employment de-
rives from a study of first year students in 11 case study schools conducted in 2002 and 2003 (as part of research conducted for the NCCA).
The figures suggest relatively high levels of employment among such
students aged, on average, 12 and 13 years. Over one-in-seven 12- and
13-year-olds worked part time in Sept of their first year in second level,
with one-in-five first years aged over 13 years similarly working. Levels
of employment had risen to a quarter by May of their first year, a considerable rise over the course of the year.

2.2.2: Participation across school years

Figure 2.4 and Table 2.1 below examine the prevalence of part-time employment across year groups, drawing on the 2001 survey. The results
suggest that levels of employment rise steadily over the junior cycle,
reaching a peak in fifth year and Transition Year, with employment falling
off slightly for the final examination year. In addition, participation in
regular paid employment rises over the second-level years, while the share
of more irregular, casual employment falls. The figures also suggest
somewhat greater levels of employment among females, partly reflecting
their greater tendency to engage in less regular babysitting-type jobs.

Figure 2.4: Participation in part-time work by school year

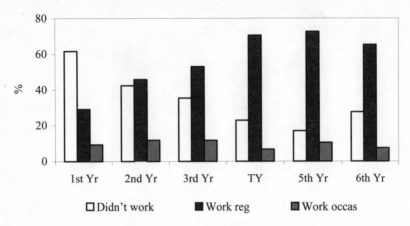

☐ Didn't work   ■ Work reg   ■ Work occas

Source: Schools Survey, 2001.

Table 2.1: Students' previous and current participation in part-time employment by school year

		1st Yr	2nd Yr	3rd Yr	TY	5th Yr	6th Yr
Males	Worked regularly	23.6	36.5	42.6	77.8	68.4	62.6
	Worked occasionally	5.2	8.8	9.1	6.3	9.8	3.7
	Didn't work	71.2	54.7	48.4	15.9	21.8	33.7
Females	Worked regularly	33.1	52.4	60.5	59.5	75.4	66.8
	Worked occasionally	12.4	14	13.4	7.1	10.9	9.9
	Didn't work	54.4	33.5	26.1	33.3	13.7	23.4
Total	Worked regularly	29.0	45.7	53	70.5	72.6	65.1
	Worked occasionally	9.3	11.8	11.6	6.7	10.5	7.4
	Didn't work	61.7	42.5	35.4	22.9	17.0	27.5

Source: Schools Survey, 2001.

Participation in paid employment over the school career can also be examined using the Annual School Leavers' Survey of 2002. Respondents were asked whether they had worked in each of the school years from first to Leaving Certificate year. Figure 2.5 indicates that participation increases from junior to senior cycle, with particularly high levels of employment in Transition Year (TY). Male levels of employment are higher than female levels throughout the junior cycle years: the induction of males into part-time work appears to be earlier than for females. In contrast, females are more likely to be employed during TY, fifth and Leaving Certificate years; perhaps owing to their high levels of take-up of babysitting-type jobs during these years.

Figure 2.5: Paid employment by school year

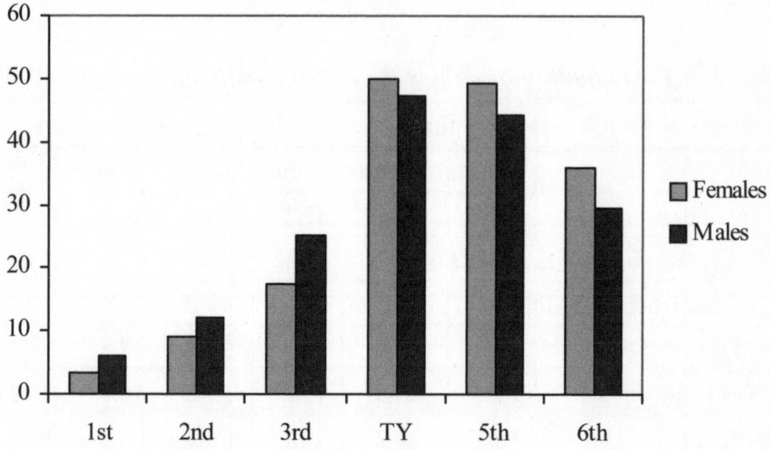

Source: Annual School Leavers' Survey, 2002

Students who had taken part in Transition Year were more likely than TY non-participants to work in fifth or sixth year. In 1999, 48 per cent of TY participants worked in fifth year compared with 35 per cent of non-participants. This difference narrowed somewhat in the Leaving Certificate year with 40 per cent of TY participants working compared with 33 per cent of non-participants. On closer investigation, this is due to the greater tendency of TY students to engage in part-time employment (see Figure 2.5 above). Eighty-three per cent of those who worked during TY continue to work in fifth year while 64 per cent continue to work in sixth year. However, students who took part in TY but did not work part-time are actually less likely than TY non-participants to work in fifth year.

2.3: INTENSITY, DAYS WORKED AND TYPE OF JOB

Table 2.2 shows the proportion of Junior and Leaving Cert students in a nationally representative sample working part-time in 1994. Unfortunately, no data were available on the days worked by these students. A quarter of all Junior Cert students worked part-time compared with 31 per cent of Leaving Cert students and employment was more prevalent among males than females. Eight per cent of Junior and Leaving Cert students were working very long hours (more than twenty hours a week) with employment intensity being significantly greater for male than female students.

Table 2.2: Participation in paid work and intensity of employment

	Junior Cert			Leaving Cert		
	Male	*Female*	*Total*	*Male*	*Female*	*Total*
Worked part-time	28.8	21.5	25.1	34.3	28.4	31.2
Of those working, hours worked						
Less than 6 hours	18.6	38.6	27.4	14.0	23.6	18.6
6–10 hours	38.5	42.3	40.2	37.5	47.5	42.3
11–15 hours	19.8	9.3	15.2	20.5	16.4	18.6
16–20 hours	11.3	6.2	9.1	16.3	8.2	12.4
More than 20 hours	11.8	3.6	8.2	11.7	4.3	8.1
Mean number of hours worked (of those working part-time)	12.1	8.4	10.5	13.0	9.5	11.3
Proportion working > 20 hrs weekly (of those working part-time)	11.8	3.6	8.2	11.7	4.3	8.1

Source: Schools Database, 1994

Drawing on the Annual School Leavers' Survey for 2002, over 58 per cent of all school leavers participated in some form of part-time employment while at school, with little variation between males and females (Table 2.3). Of those engaging in work, over half were employed during the school week and 35 per cent worked at least 15 hours weekly. The intensity of employment was slightly higher among males: with 38 per cent of males in employment working at least 15 hours weekly, relative to 32 per cent of females. Females are also less likely to be engaged in work during the school week: it appears females may be more conscious of the potential negative impact of their employment and confine their work to the weekends in an attempt to minimise any negative impact on their school activities and ultimately examination performance.

Table 2.3: Participation in part-time work: Days worked and intensity of employment

Participation in Part-Time Work	Total	Males	Females
Yes	58.1	57.0	59.1
No	41.9	43.0	40.9
Of those working, days worked			
Sat/Sun and Weekdays	49.7	51.6	48.0
Sat/Sun Only	45.3	42.6	47.9
Weekdays Only	4.9	5.8	4.1
Of those working, hours worked			
Less than 6 hours	5.1	3.5	6.6
6–10 hours	34.3	36.3	32.5
11–15 hours	25.7	22.1	29.0
16 – 20 hours	23.7	27.3	20.4
More than 20 hours	11.1	10.8	11.5
Mean Number of hours worked (of those working part-time)	14.3	14.3	13.7
Proportion working > 20 hrs weekly (of those working part-time)	11.1	10.8	11.5

Source: School Leavers' Survey 2002

It is clear from the above analyses that not only has the overall prevalence of part-time employment increased among exam year students but that the intensity of their involvement has grown, with higher proportions of students now working more than 15, if not more than twenty, hours per week. The activity of part-time employment has gone from a minority to majority pursuit among second-level students. This raises important questions about the enforcement of legislation which is designed to prohibit such excessive employment among students, particularly those aged 15 years and younger.

2.4: CHARACTERISTICS OF WORKING STUDENTS

2.4.1: Gender, region and educational characteristics

Drawing on all three data sources, it is possible to examine some of the characteristics of those who engage in part-time work and how they differ from those who do not work. Among the indicators that can be considered are gender, region, parental employment and educational attainment. Although all of these indictors cannot be examined simultaneously for any one of the data sources, they can be examined for at least one data source.

At a crude descriptive level, employment rates appear to be higher among students pursuing a vocational Leaving Certificate option, most notably the Applied Leaving Certificate (LCA) (Figure 2.6). This probably relates to the types of students pursuing the different Leaving Cert programmes, rather than effects of the programmes themselves.

Figure 2.6: Participation in part-time work at time of survey by type of senior cycle programme

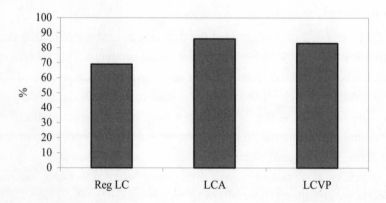

Source: Schools Survey, 2001.

Table 2.4: Educational attainment and participation in part-time work

	% Worked	% Worked >20 Hours (of those working)	% Worked Weekdays (of those working)
Second-level Attainment			
No Quals	19.3	7.4	58.7
Junior Cert	40.9	13.6	60.6
Leaving Cert	48.1	11.6	43.1
Leaving Cert with PLC/VPT	59.0	14.9	52.6
Curricular Type at School			
Vocational	52.1	15.0	49.2
Academic	47.0	10.7	46.9
Leaving Certificate Programme			
Leaving Cert	50.0	11.6	45.8
Leaving Cert Vocational Programme	53.9	18.5	38.3
Applied Leaving Cert	61.1	17.4	74.7

Source: School Leavers' Survey, 1999.

More detailed modelling of the gender, social class, regional and performance/ability characteristics of workers is presented in section 2.5.

2.4.2: Attitudinal differences between working and non-working students

The previous section has outlined the differences in some objective characteristics between working and non-working students. This section explores whether the two groups differ in their orientation to school. Because attitudes to school and whether a student was working part-time or not were measured at the same point in time, it is not appropriate to use attitudinal characteristics to *predict* the probability of working part-time as is done with objective characteristics (see below). However, it is useful to outline potential attitudinal differences between workers and non-workers as attitudes to school are likely to influence outcomes such as drop-out and performance (see Chapter Five).

The 1994 survey contained very detailed information on student attitudes and orientation to school. Students with a part-time job were found to have significantly lower educational aspirations than those who were not working (see Table 2.5). However, the direction of the relationship may be complex: do students with lower aspirations seek out employment as a bridge into the labour market or does involvement in part-time work in itself depress educational aspirations?

Table 2.5: Part-time work and educational aspirations

	Junior Cert		Leaving Cert	
Aspirations	*Working*	*Not working*	*Working*	*Not working*
Junior Cert	24.5	18.4	2.0	1.3
Leaving Cert	28.8	28.0	23.9	16.6
Cert/Diploma	26.4	27.5	43.1	35.2
Degree	20.3	26.1	31.0	47.0
Chi sq	*p<.001*		*p<.001*	

* p<.05, ** p<.01, *** p<.001

Source: Schools Database, 1994.

The two groups of students also differed in their experiences of, and orientation towards, school. Working students tended to report higher levels of negative interaction with teachers (Table 2.6). However, at Junior Certificate level working students also reported somewhat higher levels of positive interaction with teachers than their counterparts. At Junior Certificate level, working students were less likely to agree with the statement "for the most part, school life is a happy one for me". No such relationship was apparent at Leaving Certificate level, however. In addition, at Junior Certificate level working students tended to have somewhat poorer attendance records than non-working students. At Leaving Certificate level, working students tended to have more negative views of their own abilities than non-working students.

Table 2.6: Part-time work and attitudes to school

	Junior Cert		Leaving Cert	
	Working	*Not Working*	*Working*	*Not Working*
Academic self-image (mean)	2.64	2.65	2.60***	2.66
Positive teacher interaction (mean)	2.26*	2.22	2.15	2.14
Negative teacher interaction (mean)	2.18***	2.07	2.13***	2.05
Agree/strongly agree: school life happy (%)	71.0**	73.6	24.0	22.0
Good attendance (%)	73.6***	77.8	—	—

* p<.05, ** p<.01, *** p<.001. *Source*: Schools Database, 1994.

Less detailed information on student attitudes was available in the 2001 survey. It should also be noted that the students surveyed in 2001 were from six schools only and may not reflect the full range of student attitudes to school. However, some differences between working and non-working students are suggested (Table 2.7). Working students are more likely than non-working students to say they are likely to look for a job immediately or do an apprenticeship or other vocational training and less likely to say they will go on to third-level education. The aspirations of babysitters fall between the two groups. Secondly, non-working students have a more positive view of their own abilities than working students. However, the two groups do not differ in whether they find school life a happy one, in finding schoolwork interesting or in preferring not to be in school.

Table 2.7: Post-school plans by employment status (%)

	Not working	Babysitter	Other Job
Look for job	8.8	11.3	11.3
Apprenticeship	7.1	4.5	15.5
Vocational course	1.8	6.5	8.5
Third-level education	82.3	77.7	64.7
N	*283*	*247*	*433*

Source: Schools Survey, 2001.

In sum, the main "subjective" differences between working and non-working students lie in the higher educational aspirations found among non-working students. The extent to which these differences between workers and non-workers may explain potential differences in drop-out and performance will be discussed in Chapter Five.

2.5: PREDICTING THE PROBABILITY OF WORKING

This section draws on all three data sources to identify the student characteristics associated with working part-time while at school.

The Schools Database contains information collected on participation in part-time employment among Junior and Leaving Certificate students during the spring term of their exam year (1994). As outlined previously, a quarter of the Junior Certificate students and 31 per cent of the Leaving Certificate students had a job at the time of the survey (Figure 2.1). Table 2.8 presents a multivariate model predicting the type of students holding part-time jobs. In contrast to the pattern for more recent years, male students were then more likely to work part-time than their female counterparts. At Junior Certificate level, there is no systematic variation by social class background in employment participation. However, at Leaving Certificate level those from a higher professional background were much less likely to have a part-time job. At Junior Certificate level, those with neither parents employed were less likely than those with one employed parent to have a part-time job. This links with work undertaken by "The Paisley Group" in Scotland which indicates that relative deprivation is often an obstacle to, rather than a facilitator of, paid work for school age children (Mizen, Bolton and Pole, 1999). However, this pattern was not significant at Leaving Certificate level. Employment levels were much higher among students living in a dual-earner household, a pattern that was evident at both Junior and Leaving Certificate levels. This may be attributable to greater access to employment networks among this group of students. The dual-earner effect appears to be stronger for females than for males (Table 2.9).

Table 2.8: Participation in part-time work at time of the survey

	Junior Cert		Leaving Cert	
	Model 1	*Model 2*	*Model 1*	*Model 2*
Constant	6.399***	–5.012***	–2.296*	–1.125
Male	0.291***	0.307***	0.216***	0.135*
Parental class:				
Higher prof.	–0.189	–0.048	0.555***	–0.245
Lower prof.	0.163	0.247*	–0.108	0.096
Other non-manual	0.088	0.137	0.036	0.147
Skilled manual	–0.018	0.002	0.203	0.207
(Base: semi/unskill man)				
Parental employment:				
Neither employed	0.352***	–0.393***	–0.072	–0.143
Both employed	0.211**	0.222***	0.158*	0.182*
(Base: one parent employed)				
Region of school:				
East	–0.150	–0.214	0.253*	0.193
North-East	0.339*	0.342*	0.376*	0.320
North-West	–0.069	–0.192	0.163	0.118
Midlands	0.155	0.052	0.258	0.172
Mid-West	0.034	0.049	0.133	0.102
South-West	0.026	0.014	0.158	0.151
South-East	0.157	0.131	0.449**	0.378*
(Base: West)				
Age at time of survey	0.334***	0.271***	0.067	0.040
Ability test score		–0.011***		
JC grade point average				–0.094***
N	*5740*	*5740*	*4702*	*4662*
Pseudo R²	*0.034*	*0.046*	*0.025*	*0.064*

Note: unweighted data; dummy variables included for missing data.

* p<.05, ** p<.01, *** p<.001. *Source*: Schools Database, 1994.

At Junior Certificate level, there is little systematic regional variation in employment participation, although levels are significantly higher in the North-East than elsewhere. For males, employment levels are highest in the Midlands, North-East, South-East, and Mid-West, all else being equal (Table 2.9). At Leaving Certificate level, employment rates tend to be higher in eastern regions (the East, North-East and South-East) than in the West. At Junior Certificate level, older students are significantly more likely to have a part-time job than their younger counterparts. This appears to reflect legal constraints on employment for the youngest students, as no such age effect is evident at Leaving Certificate level. Students who have higher prior ability/performance levels are less likely to have a part-time job than other students.

Table 2.9: Participation in part-time work — males and females

	Junior Cert		Leaving Cert	
	Males	*Females*	*Males*	*Females*
Constant	−6.033***	−3.695***	−1.855	0.214
Parental class:				
Higher professional	−0.056	−0.066	−0.174	−0.327
Lower professional	0.376**	0.067	0.189	−0.021
Other non-manual	0.171	0.069	0.340*	−0.036
Skilled manual	0.087	−0.120	0.186	0.249
(Base: semi/unskill man)				
Parental employment:				
Neither employed	−0.422**	−0.328*	−0.274	−0.054
Both employed	0.161	0.293**	0.150	0.208*
(Base: one parent employed)				
Region of school:				
East	0.120	−0.365*	−0.204	0.466**
North-East	0.747**	0.109	−0.107	0.720**
North-West	0.114	−0.328	−0.208	0.316
Midlands	0.550*	−0.253	0.090	0.147
Mid-West	0.527*	−0.250	−0.110	0.217
South-West	0.353	−0.144	0.012	0.150
South-East	0.594*	−0.311	0.273	0.176
(Base: West)				
Age at time of survey	0.344***	0.184*	0.109	−0.050
Ability test score	−0.015***	−0.006		
JC grade point average			−0.116***	−0.075***
N	*2813*	*2927*	*2208*	*2454*
Pseudo R²	*0.062*	*0.031*	*0.085*	*0.056*

Note: unweighted data; dummy variables included for missing data.

* p<.05, ** p<.01, *** p<.001. *Source*: Schools Database, 1994.

Examining the 1999 Annual School Leavers' Survey, participation in part-time employment while at school is higher among those with both parents in employment and lower among those from the professional classes. Relative to those attending schools in the West, those from East, North-East, South-East and South-Western areas are considerably more likely to be engaged in paid employment while at school (Table 2.10).

Table 2.10: Probability of working part-time and working greater than 20 hours weekly while at school

	Probability of Working	Probability of Working > 20 Hours weekly
Constant	−4.30***	−6.20***
Male	0.03	0.30
Parental Social Class:		
Higher Professional	−0.34*	−0.39
Lower Professional	−0.25*	−0.71*
Other non-manual	0.04	−0.11
Skilled manual (Base: semi/unskilled manual)	0.21	0.32
Parental Employment:		
Neither Employed	0.21	−0.30
Both Employed (Base: one parent employed)	0.23*	0.29
Region While at School:		
East	1.22***	1.52**
North-East	1.10***	0.58
North-West	0.27	1.09
Midlands	0.09	1.30*
Mid-West	0.46*	1.19*
South-West	0.95***	1.55**
South-East	0.99***	1.46*
(Base: West)		
Age in years at time of survey	0.18***	0.10

* $p<.05$, ** $p<.01$, *** $p<.001$

Source: School Leavers' Survey, 1999

Working more than 20 hours per week also shows strong regional variation controlling for gender and social background characteristics: those
from the Eastern seaboard, the South-West and the Midlands are significantly more likely to work more than 20 hours per week than those from
the West. There are no significant gender differences in terms of the
probability of working or the probability of working long hours.

In sum, there appears to be a growth over time in the importance of
social background factors. In particular, social class and parental employment effects appear to become stronger over time. Engagement in
part-time work activities, particularly more regular and time-intensive
employment, while at school is significantly less prevalent among more
economically advantaged students and this pattern has become more pronounced over the seven years covered by the data. If part-time work has
any negative effects on student outcomes, it may therefore be acting to
reinforce existing social inequalities.

2.6: SUMMARY

Results across the three data sources illustrate the growing importance
over time of part-time work activities among second-level students. Participation levels rise over the school career, reaching a peak in Transition
Year. Employment levels also appear to be higher among those pursuing
vocational Leaving Cert options: the Applied and Vocational Leaving
Certificate programmes.

Workers are found to differ in both their "objective" characteristics,
including gender, social background and regional characteristics, and
also in their subjective attitudes towards school. Overall females are
more likely to be in employment. However, when less regular informal
jobs (largely babysitting) are excluded, males are more likely to be in
employment and are significantly more likely to occupy jobs with greater
time commitments and which entail weekday work. There is some evidence of lower employment levels among students in western areas, relative to those from the eastern regions: this may relate to the availability
and accessibility of "student jobs". Over time the role of social class factors becomes more apparent: those from professional and intermediate
non-manual backgrounds are less likely to be working, with the most

affluent particularly less likely to work long hours. In addition, the most recent survey data indicate employment levels in the most intensive jobs are highest among those with neither parent in employment.

In terms of more subjective measures, workers are found to have lower educational aspirations and tend to report higher levels of negative interaction with teachers. In addition, working students are less likely to be happy with school life and are likely to have poorer attendance records (at Junior Certificate level) and have more negative views of their abilities (at Leaving Certificate level).

Chapter Three

MOTIVATION FOR WORKING

3.1: INTRODUCTION

S tudents' motivations for engaging in part-time work while at school are the subject of Chapter 3, an area which has received little attention to date in the Irish context. Among the issues examined are the reasons for working and, among those who do not engage in this activity, the reasons for not working. In addition, the role of parental and school attitudes in working decisions and the role of parental financial support are examined. The expenditure patterns of young people are also reviewed. Finally, the occupational aspirations of "workers" and the role of part-time work in fostering or promoting longer-term occupational aspirations are considered. Most notably, the question of whether they aspire to continued employment in their field of work or whether their aspirations lie elsewhere and current work is viewed as a temporary, short-term source of income is examined. Results presented in this chapter are based solely on the 2001 survey.

3.2: REASONS FOR NOT WORKING

In considering the restrictions on students' working, overall 45 per cent of those not working would work if they had the choice; the figure is 55 per cent at Junior Certificate level and 32 per cent at Leaving Certificate level.

Concern over school grades constitutes the strongest deterrent to working part-time (Figure 3.1a): this concern is considerably stronger among females and among those at Leaving Certificate level (Figures 3.1b and 3.1c). The latter is expected but the former suggests a greater level of awareness among girls of the possible negative repercussions of such employment on examination performance.

The role of alternative financial resources are also strong in not working: almost 60 per cent consider that they receive adequate pocket money from their parents and 36 per cent have saved sufficient money from summer work to offset the need to work during the school term. A sizable proportion (40 per cent) mention that they have no desire to work part-time; this is also higher among girls and Leaving Certificate students.

Finally, an inability to find a job or a suitable job is mentioned by 40 per cent as a factor in their not working. As might be expected given legal constraints on the employment of younger students, this difficulty is greater among the younger Junior Certificate group. It is also somewhat higher among girls, who are particularly more likely to cite a difficulty in finding "suitable" employment.

Figure 3.1a: Main reasons for not working part-time

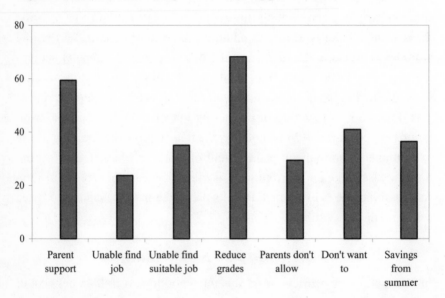

Source: Schools Survey, 2001.

Figure 3.1b: Main reasons for not working part-time — males and females

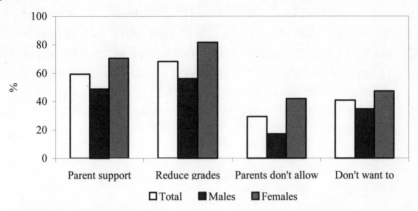

Source: Schools Survey, 2001.

Figure 3.1c: Main reasons for not working part-time — Junior and Leaving Cert

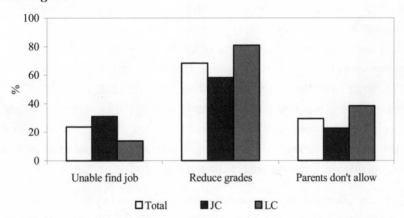

Source: Schools Survey, 2001.

3.3: PARENTAL AND SCHOOL APPROVAL/DISAPPROVAL

Overall 23 per cent of students indicate that their parents disapprove of part-time work: this figure is 15 per cent for those with jobs and 43 per cent for those not working. While over 43 per cent of those not working feel their parents disapprove, only 30 per cent state that they don't work for this reason.

A majority of students consider their school does not approve of part-time work (56 per cent), however this varies across the six schools (ranging from 39 per cent to 63 per cent). Interestingly, the school where students are most likely to report school disapproval of part-time work also has the highest levels of participation in employment. Overall, levels of employment are slightly lower among students who maintain their school does not approve of such practices (67 per cent employed relative to 75 per cent employed among those who contend that their school does not disapprove).

3.4: EXPENDITURE PATTERNS[1]

The single biggest item of expenditure is entertainment, mentioned by nearly three-quarters of students as something they spend a lot or quite a lot of their income on (Figure 3.2a). Expenditure on clothes/shoes and CDs/music also figure prominently. Almost a third cite alcohol as an area of significant expenditure and 17 per cent mention cigarettes. A mere 3 per cent mention the family budget as an area of substantial expenditure. Boys are more likely to report spending on alcohol (37 per cent of boys relative to 27 per cent of girls), while girls more frequently mention clothes/shoes and cigarettes (Figure 3.2b). Some differences also emerge between the two age cohorts. Expenditure on alcohol and entertainment is reported more frequently among the Leaving Certificate group; age restrictions may curtail these activities for the younger Junior Certificate group (Figure 3.2c). Our findings regarding patterns of student expenditure support earlier research that concludes:

> Overwhelmingly the motivation for students to mix work and study is to earn more money. In the large majority of cases this appears to be to maintain a preferred lifestyle, rather than as a result of financial hardship. Deprivation does not appear to be a major factor (Davies, 1999).

---

[1] The survey did not ask about expenditure on mobile phones, but it is likely that this would also represent an area of considerable expenditure.

Figure 3.2a: Expenditure on various items

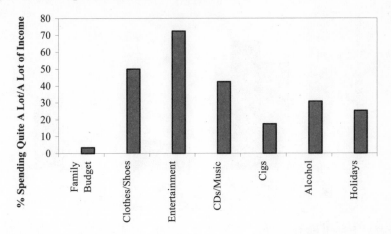

Source: Schools Survey, 2001.

Figure 3.2b: Expenditure patterns of boys and girls

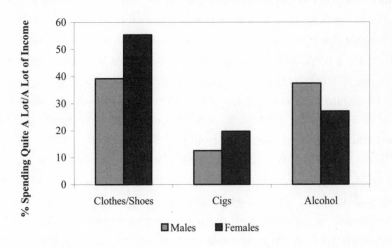

Source: Schools Survey, 2001.

Figure 3.2c: Expenditure patterns of Junior and Leaving Cert students

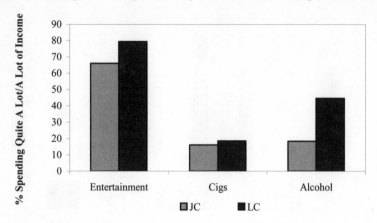

Source: Schools Survey, 2001.

3.5: POST-SCHOOL ASPIRATIONS

Plans to progress to third-level education show some relationship to part-time work participation; this issue is examined more thoroughly in Chapter 5 where the effects of part-time work participation are modelled controlling for a range of background factors associated with the propensity to engage in work. Suffice to say, at the descriptive level, those engaging in paid employment are less likely to aspire to third-level education (as noted in Chapter 2). This holds at both Junior and Leaving Certificate levels and for boys and girls: for example, while 87 per cent of Leaving Certificate boys not working part-time plan to progress to third-level education, only 57 per cent of those who are in part-time employment have similar plans. Overall, as illustrated in Figure 3.3, 82 per cent of non-workers, 70 per cent of all those working part-time and 51 per cent of those engaged in working more than twenty hours a week aspire to third-level education.

Figure 3.3: Post-school expectations of working and non-working students

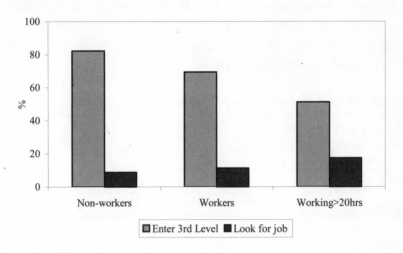

Source: Schools Survey, 2001.

3.5.1: Aspirations to continue in same/similar job

One-third of those engaged in part-time employment consider it likely that they will work in the same job or a similar job when they have left school (Table 3.1). Plans to continue in the same/similar job are slightly more common among boys, particularly at the Leaving Certificate level. This is partly explained by those working in non-babysitting type jobs, in which boys are more highly represented, being more likely to aspire to continue in the same job; while 31 per cent of those working in babysitting plan to continue in this domain, the figure for those working in other areas is 35 per cent. Table 3.2 displays occupational aspirations accord- ing to type of job: plans to continue in the same or similar job are higher among those engaged in farming, factory and pub/off-licence work than in other kinds of work.

Not surprisingly, there appears to be some relationship between plans to continue in a similar job and post-school plans more generally: while one-fifth of those who plan to continue in similar job also plan to look for a job straight away, only 7 per cent of those not planning to continue in the same job have similar post-school job search aspirations. Conversely aspirations to progress to higher education are considerably higher among those not planning to continue working in a similar job. Finally, those who intend to work in a similar job after leaving school are also significantly more likely to consider that their job enables them to learn new skills (almost 90 per cent) than those who do not plan to work in a similar job (three-quarters).

Table 3.1: Plans to work in same or similar job after leaving school

Likely or Very Likely to work in same or similar job when leave school?	JC		LC		Total
	Males	*Females*	*Males*	*Females*	
Likely or very likely	36.5	33.2	40.2	29.7	33.9
Not likely	63.5	66.8	59.8	70.3	66.1

Table 3.2: Proportion who plan to continue in same/similar job by type of job

	Males	Females	Total
Farming	54.5	*	53.8
Factory	43.1	*	44.6
Clerical	*	*	43.8
Petrol station/shop	25.0	19.4	21.3
Pub/off-licence	48.6	43.1	45.2
Hotel/restaurant	*	*	7.7
Babysitting	32.1	32.1	32.1
Other	*	*	41.7

* Small numbers

Source: Schools Survey, 2001.

3.6: SUMMARY

Students who make the decision not to engage in part-time employment while at school are overwhelmingly motivated by a concern about grades and examination performance. The role of parental support is also central. The concern about grades is particularly strong among girls, who appear more cognisant of the demands of school, and Leaving Certificate students for whom the demands of the impending State exam are more immediate. Financial support from home and the reserves from summer work are also facilitators in enabling young people to decide not to work. There is some evidence that an inability to find a job is a factor among the younger Junior Cert cohort: this may indicate a responsiveness among employers to age restrictions in the employment of young people (*Protection of Young Persons Act, 1996*; see Chapter One).

The majority of workers spend a considerable portion of their income on entertainment, while spending on alcohol, particularly among boys, and clothes/shoes and cigarettes, more frequently among girls, are also prominent areas of expenditure.

Regarding job aspirations, considerable proportions aspire to continue in similar jobs after leaving school: this being more prevalent among boys and those working in farming, factory and pub/off-licence fields.

Workers are significantly less likely than non-workers to perceive that their parents or their school disapprove of part-time work. However, the direction of causality is unclear: do students respond to their parents and school views or are parents and schools reacting to high levels of student employment?

Chapter Four

"QUALITY" AND INTENSITY OF WORK

4.1: INTRODUCTION

Chapter 4 reviews the nature and "quality" of jobs in which students engage. This includes an examination of the regularity and hours of work, the type of occupation and industry in which they are employed, pay levels and whether they are included in the tax net or engage in informal activities such as babysitting. It is based on analysis of the 2001 survey.

4.2: TYPE OF WORK

Some consideration is now given to the type of work students are engaged in and to what extent these jobs vary among different groups of students (Figure 4.1). This issue is important in so far as it relates to the nature of the work: in particular, whether the work is structured and perhaps related to schoolwork or school activities or unstructured with little linkage to school. It also throws some light on the demands or flexibilities of the work and whether such work is likely to impinge on school and social activities. The type of work undertaken by students might also play a role in their later labour market experiences and their ability to find a "good" job. The 2001 survey indicates an overwhelming concentration of students in service sector jobs: most notably petrol stations/shops (21 per cent), pubs/off-licences (14 per cent) and the hotel/restaurant/fast-food sector (4 per cent), with these jobs accounting for 40 per cent of the jobs students are engaged in. A similar proportion are employed in less structured babysitting-type jobs, while a further 10 per cent are employed in factories and 6 per cent in farm activities.

Figure 4.1: Types of work engaged in by gender and school year

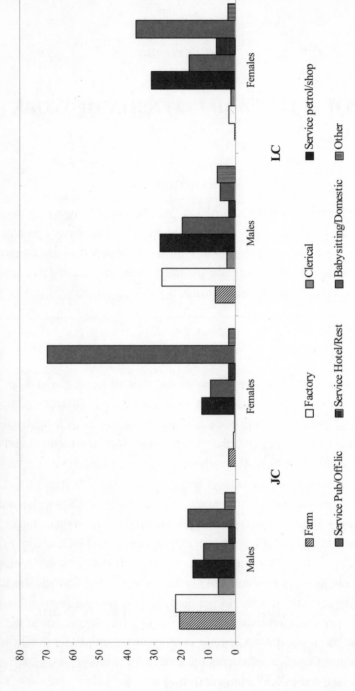

Girls are strongly over-represented in domestic or babysitting-type jobs, particularly the younger Junior Certificate girls, 70 per cent of whom are employed as babysitters. Participation in the more formal services sector is more prominent among the older Leaving Certificate cohort (accounting for over half of Leaving Certificate workers, relative to a quarter of the Junior Certificate group): this may be partly related to legal restrictions on the employment of young persons, particularly those aged under 18 years (*Protection of Young Persons Employment Act, 1996*). Conversely, males are more likely to be engaged in farming activities, accounting for a fifth of Junior Certificate males and 7 per cent of their Leaving Certificate counterparts. In addition, males, particularly those at Leaving Cert level, are more highly represented in factory work. Thus, the younger cohort is more prominent in the less formal farming and domestic sectors while the older students are more likely to be employed in the more formal factory and shop/pub setting.

4.3: PARTICIPATION IN UNPAID EMPLOYMENT

Unpaid work, taking the form of assistance on the family farm or family business, is reported by an eighth of students. These activities are slightly more common among males than females (16 per cent for males and 10 per cent for females) with gender differences being more pronounced among the older Leaving Certificate cohort; 14 per cent of males and 10 per cent of females at Junior Certificate engaged in unpaid family work compared with 20 per cent of males and 10 per cent of females at Leaving Certificate level. Males tend to work longer hours, working an average of 13 hours in unpaid duties relative to 7 hours for females. There is some evidence of a trade-off with paid work: 11 per cent of those with paid jobs are also engaged in unpaid work relative to 17 per cent of those without paid employment. The issue of involvement in domestic work is taken up in Chapter 5.

4.4: REGULARITY AND INTENSITY OF WORK

Girls are more likely than boys to confine their work to the weekends as are Leaving Certificate students relative to their Junior Certificate counterparts (see Table 4.1). However, in terms of regularity of work, Leaving Certificate students are more likely to be engaged in regular weekly jobs, while those at Junior Certificate are more likely to work less regularly, reflecting their over-representation in babysitting-type employment. In addition, males are more likely to be working regularly and females on a more ad hoc basis, again relating to their greater representation in childcare-type work (Table 4.2).

Table 4.1: Days worked in week among those engaged in part-time employment

	Weekend Work Only %	Weekday Work only or Both Weekday & Weekend Work %
Males	38	62
Females	53	47
Junior Cert	43	57
Leaving Cert	53	47
Total	48	52

Source: Schools Survey, 2001.

Table 4.2: Regularity of work among those engaged in part-time employment

	Weekly %	Less Regularly %
Males	76	24
Females	66	34
Junior Cert	65	35
Leaving Cert	75	25
Total	70	30

Source: Schools Survey, 2001.

At both Junior and Leaving Certificate levels, boys work longer hours than girls. The difference is most pronounced at the most intensive levels of employment: while 23 per cent of Leaving Cert boys in employment work more than 20 hours weekly, the figure for girls is just 12 per cent. Conversely, girls are substantially more likely to engage in employment that accounts for less than 10 hours per week. There is some evidence from international research that highly intensive jobs are most detrimental in terms of academic and educational outcomes, an issue which is examined in Chapter Five.

The extent to which this gender difference reflects differences in the type of work being pursued by boys and girls is examined in Table 4.4. Jobs carrying the most time-intensive commitments are located in the farming, factory and pub/off-licence sectors, with farming and factory work predominantly occupied by males. Conversely, babysitting jobs are the least time-intensive. To illustrate, over one-quarter of those employed in the farming, factory and pub/off-licence spheres are working at least 20 hours weekly, while just 11 per cent of those engaged in babysitting duties are working similar hours. Similarly, employment during the school week is less frequent among more typically female babysitting jobs, while employment in a petrol station/shop, farm, factory or pub/off-licence are more likely to entail weekday work commitments.

Table 4.3: Hours worked among those working part-time

	Junior Cert		Leaving Cert		Total
	Males	*Females*	*Males*	*Females*	
1 to 9 Hours	35.9	49.0	21.7	41.4	39.7
10–15 Hours	27.4	29.2	29.6	31.5	29.7
16–20 Hours	16.2	10.7	26.1	14.8	15.4
21 or more	20.5	11.1	22.6	12.3	15.1
Mean hours worked	15.1	11.6	16.4	13.0	13.5

Source: Schools Survey, 2001.

Table 4.4: Hours and days worked by type of job

	Mean Hours Worked	% Working at Least 20 Hours	% Working Weekdays
Farming	16.1	27.5	58.3
Factory	17.0	25.8	55.6
Clerical	12.8	20.0	46.7
Petrol station/shop	15.0	20.7	59.4
Pub/off-licence	15.6	26.0	51.2
Hotel/restaurant	14.6	14.8	37.5
Babysitting	10.7	11.3	47.3
Other	12.7	16.7	65.0
Total	13.5	18.2	52.1

Source: Schools Survey, 2001.

4.5: PAY AND PAYMENT OF TAX/PRSI

Overall males receive higher hourly earnings for their part-time employment (Tables 4.5 and 4.6). At Junior Cert males receive 1.3 times the earnings of females, while at Leaving Cert they earn nearly 1.4 times more. When informal jobs relating to babysitting are excluded, males are still in an advantageous position, although the gender pay gap is less pronounced. In addition, with the exception of hotel/restaurant and clerical jobs, males receive higher hourly earnings in all areas of employment (Figure 4.2).

Table 4.5: Average earnings of male and female students (€ per hour)

	Males	Females	Total	Ratio
Junior Cert Students	5.99	4.58	5.04	1.31
Leaving Cert Students	7.86	5.66	6.49	1.39
Total	6.93	5.07	5.71	1.37

Source: Schools Survey, 2001.

*Table 4.6: Average earnings of male and female students (€ per hour),
excluding "babysitting" jobs*

	Males	**Females**	**Total**	**Ratio**
Junior Cert Students	6.22	5.59	5.94	1.10
Leaving Cert Students	7.91	6.15	6.96	1.29
Total	7.12	5.94	6.54	1.20

Source: Schools Survey, 2001.

Figure 4.2: Hourly earnings by type of job

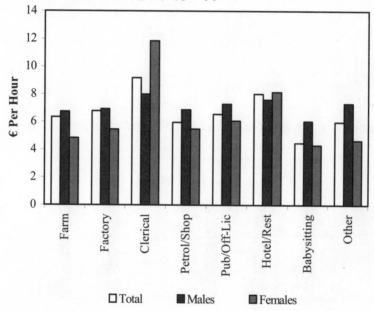

Source: Schools Survey, 2001.

Inclusion in the tax-net also shows strong gender and age variation: girls
and Junior Cert students are less likely to be paying tax, a pattern which
is related to their over-representation in informal casual jobs in the child-
care field (i.e. babysitting). While three-quarters of girls and almost 80
per cent of Junior Cert students are engaged in non-taxed employment,
the figure for boys and Leaving Cert students is just 61 per cent (Figures
4.3a and 4.3b). However, a significant proportion of student workers are
not actually aware of whether they are paying tax; this stands at approximately 15 per cent with little difference for gender and age groups.

Figure 4.3a: Payment of tax/PRSI for students holding part-time jobs

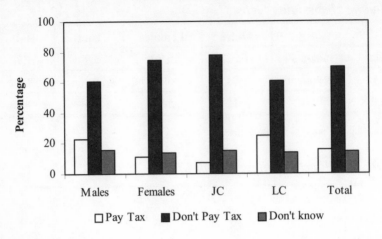

Source: Schools Survey, 2001.

Figure 4.3b: Payment of tax/PRSI for jobs excluding babysitting

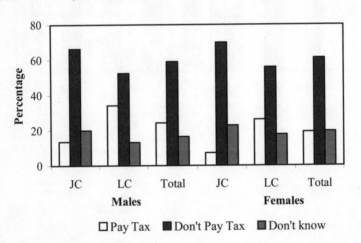

Source: Schools Survey, 2001.

4.6: PARENTAL SUPPORT AND POCKET MONEY — TRADE-OFF?

Do levels of employment vary according to receipt of pocket money and amount of money received? Does employment intensity reflect the level of financial support at home? Overall just under half of respondents receive regular pocket money, with little variation between boys and girls (Table 4.7a). Participation in part-time paid employment shows a clear relationship with receipt of pocket money: while 44 per cent of workers receive financial support from home in the form of pocket money, 56 per cent of their non-working counterparts receive such support. Interestingly, this divergence appears to operate only for boys: financial support shows a work trade-off for boys but not for girls. This may relate to the greater amounts of money being received by boys compared to girls (see above), and to the over-representation of girls in less regular babysitting-type jobs. In addition, there appears to be some variation in employment intensity according to whether students are receiving pocket money: while 35 per cent of those working at least 20 hours weekly receive pocket money, almost half of their counterparts working less than 20 hours weekly receive such assistance.

Table 4.7a: Receipt of regular "pocket money" and participation in part-time paid employment

% Receiving Regular Pocket Money	At Work Part-time	Not Working	Total
Males	40	61	48
Females	47	48	47
Total	44	56	48
Of Which:			
Working < 20 hours weekly	47		
Working at least 20 hours weekly	35		

Source: Schools Survey, 2001.

Table 4.7b: Average pocket money received per week (€)

Males	Females	Workers	Non-workers
19.7	17.5	18.5	17.9

Source: Schools Survey, 2001.

4.7: TOTAL INCOME: PAID EMPLOYMENT AND PARENTAL SUPPORT

Given the substantial proportion of workers also in receipt of parental support (in the form of pocket money), this section reviews the total amounts of income received by students in employment at second level (i.e. income from employment and regular pocket money from parents). Again males are in the advantageous position of receiving higher total income than their female counterparts, with the gender difference persisting across different levels of employment intensity (Table 4.8). Overall, males in employment on average receive €111 weekly, compared to just €66 weekly for females. Among those working 10–15 hours weekly, males receive a total income 1.4 times that of females, while among those working 16–20 hours male income is 1.5 times that of their female counterparts.

In terms of type of employment, highest total income levels appear to occur for those employed on farms and in clerical, factory, petrol station/ shop and pub/off-licence positions, with the lowest total income levels occurring among babysitters (Table 4.9). For instance, among those working at least 20 hours per week, those working on farms and in clerical positions report an average total income of €167 and €159 weekly, relative to €120 weekly reported among babysitters. Total income received by male students considerably exceeds that of females in all employment sectors (see Table 4.9).

Interestingly, the income variation between workers and non-workers is stark (Table 4.8): while workers are receiving on average €81 weekly, those not participating in employment have average income (from pocket money) of just €10 per week. As with workers, male non-workers are in receipt of higher income (i.e. parental support) than their female counterparts.

Table 4.8: Total income by hours worked and gender (€)

	Males	**Females**	**Total**	**Male:Female Ratio**
1–9 hours	48.5	39.6	41.8	1.22
10–15 hours	102.1	72.0	82.1	1.42
16–20 hours	147.2	96.4	118.7	1.53
21 or more	171.8	121.8	147.4	1.41
Average all workers	110.5	65.7	81.0	1.68
Average non-workers	10.8	8.0	9.5	1.35
Average all students	72.0	51.8	60.2	1.39

Source: Schools Survey, 2001.

Table 4.9: Total income of students in employment by type of job, year and gender (€)

	Hours Worked		**Junior Cert**		**Leaving Cert**	
	< 20 hours	*At least 20 hours*	*Males*	*Females*	*Males*	*Females*
Farming	92.4	166.5	131.0	57.3	138.3	85.1
Factory	90.0	146.2	99.4	81.0	126.5	82.9
Clerical	95.8	158.7	*	*	*	*
Petrol station/shop	79.4	152.9	115.7	60.4	129.6	90.8
Pub/off-licence	81.4	147.2	127.9	87.7	117.3	84.4
Hotel/restaurant	75.0	127.0	*	*	*	*
Babysitting	47.6	119.7	75.3	48.0	178.8	62.9
Other	69.5	104.8	*	*	*	*
Mean	67.8	141.3	103.6	55.2	127.5	77.8

* Small numbers

Source: Schools Survey, 2001.

4.8: SUMMARY

This chapter has clearly illustrated the gendered nature of employment among second-level students in Ireland. Females are considerably more likely to engage in informal babysitting-type employment, which is likely to be less time-intensive and more likely to be confined to the weekend and therefore less likely to infringe on school and homework demands. Male students are over-represented in the more formal and regular labour market jobs, particularly those pertaining to more traditional employment spheres, such as farming and factory work; they are more likely to work longer hours and work during the school week. In addition, they are more highly represented in unpaid family work, typically farm or family business, and again work longer hours in these activities. Gender differences in earnings are also apparent: males receive higher earnings at both Junior and Leaving Cert levels, even excluding informal babysitting employment; a difference which holds across almost all types of employment. Overall, students are most likely to be employed in service jobs particularly in petrol stations/shops, pubs/off-licences and the hotel/restaurant/fast-food sector.

When we also consider income from parents, i.e. pocket money, males are in a more advantageous position and, when total income is considered, males are again better off, a difference which holds when account is taken of the type of job and hours worked.

Chapter Five

PART-TIME WORK AND
STUDENT OUTCOMES

This chapter explores the relationship between working part-time while at school and a range of student outcomes. The analyses allow us to directly test whether part-time employment has positive or negative effects on outcomes such as early school leaving, examination performance and integration into employment. The first section considers the perceived and actual effects of part-time work on time spent on study and leisure activities. The second section examines patterns of school drop-out among part-time workers compared with those not engaged in paid employment. The relationship between part-time work and exam performance at both Junior and Leaving Certificate levels is explored in the third section. This section also applies statistical techniques to control for possible selection effects between the two groups, as discussed in the review of the literature in Chapter 1. The fourth section explores the relationships between part-time work, other out-of-school activities and examination performance. The fifth section analyses school-to-work transition patterns among students comparing those with work experience and those without.

5.1: PART-TIME WORK, STUDY AND LEISURE ACTIVITIES

5.1.1: The perceived effects of part-time work

In the 2001 survey, students who were engaged in paid work were asked about the effects this work had on their schoolwork. Figure 5.1 indicates that almost a third of students feel that working part-time means that they are likely to have less time for homework. However, only a minority of students consider that part-time work interferes with their schoolwork or is likely to result in them doing worse in school or missing more days from school. Those who work more than 20 hours per week are more likely to perceive their employment as having potentially negative effects on their schoolwork than those who work fewer hours. In addition, those who work as babysitters are less likely than those in a 'job' to see part-time work as having negative effects, a pattern that is likely to reflect the lower number of hours and greater flexibility of working arrangements associated with babysitting. On the whole, male students are more likely to see part-time work as having negative effects but this pattern is due to their tendency to work longer hours rather than to gender differences per se.

Figure 5.1: Perceptions of the effects of part-time work

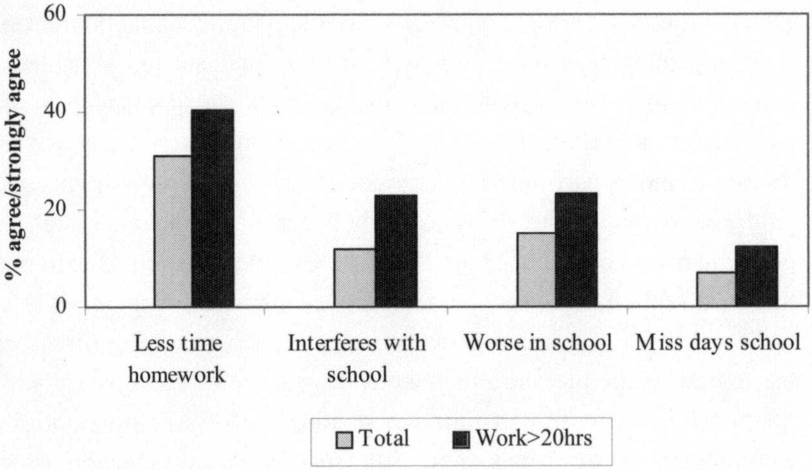

Source: Schools Survey, 2001.

Figure 5.2 indicates perceptions of the effects of part-time work by exam year. Leaving Certificate students are significantly more likely to see part-time work as interfering with their study time, their schoolwork and their school performance. These differences are apparent even when the hours spent in paid employment are controlled for and may reflect the greater workload involved in preparing for the Leaving Cert exam. Leaving Cert students are somewhat more likely than their Junior Cert counterparts to see part-time work as being likely to affect their absence from school, although this difference is not statistically significant.

Figure 5.2: Perceived effects of part-time work by exam year

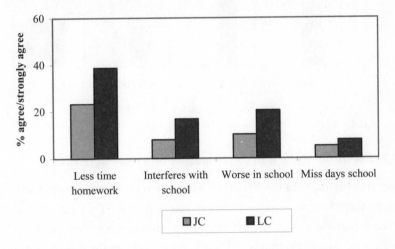

Source: Schools Survey, 2001.

In addition to allowing us to explore the perceived effects of part-time work, the 2001 survey of exam-year students in six schools allowed us to compare workers and non-workers in terms of the actual time they spent on homework and study. These patterns can also be contrasted with those found among the national sample of students in 1994.

Figure 5.3 indicates that among the 1994 cohort, those in paid employment spent significantly less time on homework and study than their non-working counterparts at both Junior and Leaving Cert levels. At first glance, the 2001 data would appear to indicate no significant difference between workers and non-workers in time spent on study. However, this is due to the different profile found among those engaged in babysitting activities who, in fact, have very high levels of time spent on homework. If this group is excluded from the worker category, those in paid employment are found to spend significantly less time on homework and study than those not working.

Figure 5.3: Time spent on homework/study (average weekday evening)
by employment status

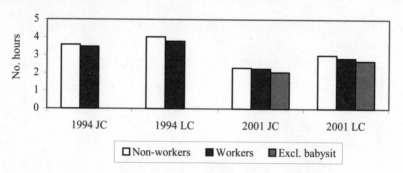

5.1.2: Part-time work and participation in leisure activities

Chapter 3 highlighted the extent to which income from part-time work is used to fund leisure activities among young people. Two-thirds of those working part-time in 2001 felt that their employment allowed them "to have more fun at weekends". This response was more common among male students and those at Leaving Cert level. However, a third of the sample felt that part-time work meant they were likely to have less time for sports and hobbies; this perception was significantly more prevalent among those working more than twenty hours a week.

The 1994 and 2001 surveys also allow us to explore actual differences in participation in different types of leisure activities between workers and non-workers (see Table 5.1).[1] Contrary to the perceptions of some respondents, there is no evidence that workers have less time for leisure activities than non-workers. In terms of participation in school-based sports, workers at Junior Cert level in 1994 were actually found to have higher involvement than non-workers. However, the pattern among Leaving Cert students in 2001 was reversed with lower participation among workers. This pattern appears to be related to gender differences in sports participation since, when babysitters are excluded from the worker category, no marked differences are found between workers and non-workers. There is

---

[1] Gender differences are evident in the level of participation in different leisure activities with boys being more likely to be involved in all of the specified activities except non-sports extracurricular activities. However, differences in participation between workers and non-workers hold within gender groups.

no significant variation between workers and non-workers in involvement in extracurricular activities (such as music, debates and plays), although levels of participation are low among both groups (Table 5.1).

The main differences between workers and non-workers relate to participation in non-school social activities. In 1994, workers were more likely to participate in non-school sports than non-workers, although this pattern is not evident in the 2001 data. Among Leaving Cert students, workers tend to spend more time watching television and on other pastimes than non-workers. Workers are more likely than non-workers to have gone to a disco, concert or the cinema, taken alcohol with friends and gone on a date three or more times in the past two weeks. The difference between workers and non-workers in their social activities is even more marked if babysitters are excluded from the worker category. In overall terms, it appears that social activity is facilitated by income from part-time work. However, greater social activity may also provide a financial motivation for obtaining part-time work in the first place. The extent to which higher levels of participation in social activity can influence student outcomes such as exam performance is discussed later in the chapter.

Workers and non-workers may also vary in their involvement in various types of unpaid work. In 2001, students in the six case-study schools were asked about helping out in the family business or farm without getting regular pay. Twelve per cent were doing this kind of unpaid work (see Chapter 4). While such work was more common among those without paid employment, it is worth noting that 11 per cent of those who worked part-time for pay also helped out in the family business. Respondents to the 2001 survey were also asked whether they had taken part in any voluntary work (such as fundraising for charity or visiting elderly people) in the two weeks prior to the survey. Under a quarter of those surveyed had taken part in such activities. However, participation in voluntary work was significantly higher among those working part-time than non-working students (26 per cent compared with 18 per cent). Differences in involvement between workers and non-workers were especially evident among Leaving Cert students. This would appear to suggest that those in part-time employment may be more socially involved overall, a pattern which has been found among older people (Fahey and Russell, 2001).

Table 5.1: Participation in leisure activities by employment and exam year

Proportion Who Took Part Three or More Times in Past Two Weeks:	1994				2001					
	Junior Cert		Leaving Cert		Junior Cert			Leaving Cert		
	Non-worker	Worker	Non-worker	Worker	Non-worker	Worker	Excl. baby-sitters	Non-worker	Worker	Excl. baby-sitters
School-based sports	**15.4**	**17.2**	13.5	14.6	20.8	16.3	18.7	19.0	10.5	13.3
Other extracurricular activities	3.7	4.5	3.5	4.8	3.9	3.3	3.7	5.0	3.6	2.7
Non-school sports	**33.6**	**42.0**	**24.3**	**30.9**	34.0	33.2	36.1	23.8	21.5	34.2
Disco/concert/cinema	**30.9**	**41.4**	**26.4**	**36.4**	25.5	36.3	36.8	29.9	36.0	38.9
Went drinking	**10.7**	**19.3**	**22.8**	**31.1**	14.5	18.5	20.3	26.8	38.4	44.3
Went on a date	**20.2**	**31.7**	**21.9**	**30.2**	21.4	30.1	33.9	29.4	32.0	35.7
Time spent on TV and other pastimes	2.34	2.43	**1.92**	**2.11**	2.81	2.77	2.76	2.35	2.55	2.62
Number of cases	5961		4813		552			462		

Note: Significant differences between workers and non-workers in 1994 at the p<.05 level are highlighted in bold.

Sources: Schools Database, 1994; Schools Survey, 2001.

Figure 5.4: Participation in household labour by gender (Junior Cert students, 1994)

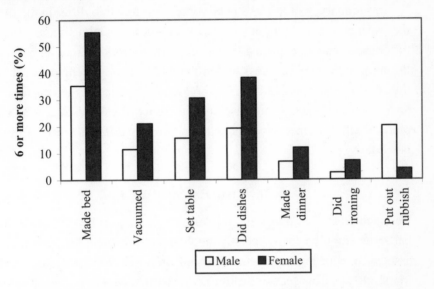

In addition, information was available from both the 1994 and 2001 surveys on the extent of student involvement in household chores. Girls have higher levels of involvement than boys in all household tasks, with the exception of bringing out the rubbish. Figure 5.4 indicates the pattern for Junior Cert students in 1994; similar patterns are found among Leaving Cert students, and among students in the case-study schools in 2001. An index of involvement in household labour was constructed summing the frequency of carrying out the specified activity for both the 1994 and 2001 surveys.[2] All else being equal, involvement in household labour is greater among girls, those with both parents or neither parent employed (compared with one parent in employment), those from larger families and those with lower ability/prior performance levels. Interestingly, in 1994 those working part-time work tended to have higher levels of involvement in household labour perhaps indicating greater independence and self-reliance among these students. Within the 2001 cohort, girls in regular jobs appear to do somewhat more housework than those without

---

[2] The 2001 survey differed from the 1994 survey in including an additional item on the frequency of looking after younger siblings.

any work while no marked difference was apparent between working and non-working male students.

In summary, workers and non-workers are found to differ in the time they spend on study and in their involvement in social activities. These differences may be expected to impact on their school career, in particular on how far they progress within the educational system and on how they perform in examinations. The following sections of the chapter use data from the Schools Database and the School Leavers' Survey to explore whether, in fact, workers and non-workers differ in terms of these outcomes.

5.2: SCHOOL DROP-OUT

Research from the American and Australian contexts has indicated that part-time employment, especially employment involving longer hours, is associated with higher levels of school drop-out (see Robinson, 1999; Marsh, 1991). This section explores whether this pattern is evident in the Irish context. Chapter 2 has indicated that workers and non-workers differ in terms of their social background, prior ability/performance, attitudes to school and educational aspirations, all factors which have been previously found to influence student drop-out and exam performance (see, for example, Smyth, 1999). It is important, therefore, that we compare "like with like" in analysing the difference between working and non-working students by controlling for background characteristics and, where possible, attitudinal factors.

The School Leavers' Survey data allowed us to explore drop-out at junior cycle level; that is, to identify young people who had left school before taking the Junior Cert exam. Because the Schools Database contained information on the Leaving Cert results of the 1994 Junior Cert cohort, it could be used to identify drop-out at senior cycle level, that is, those who left school after the Junior Cert but before the Leaving Cert exam. Because the outcome is dichotomous (students drop out before the Junior Cert or do not), a logistic regression model is used to assess the effect of the explanatory variables on the log odds of dropping out of school as opposed to remaining on in full-time education. A positive coefficient indicates increased chances of dropping out while a negative coefficient indicates reduced chances of leaving school early. Definitions of the variables used are detailed in Appendix 5.1.

Table 5.2: Part-time work and junior cycle drop-out

	Coefficient
Constant	−3.407***
Background Characteristics:	
Male	0.574*
Parental Social Class:	
Higher Professional	−2.500**
Lower Professional	−1.545***
Other non-manual	−1.345**
Skilled manual	−0.826*
(Base: semi/unskilled manual)	
Parental Employment:	
Neither Employed	0.823**
Both Employed	−0.256
(Base: one parent employed)	
Region While at School:	
East	0.274
North-East	0.666
North-West	0.880
Midlands	0.801
Mid-West	0.318
South-West	−0.957
South-East	0.140
(Base: West)	
Worked in First Year	0.901*
N	*2520*
Pseudo R^2	*0.141*

Note: *** p<.001, ** p<.01, * p<.05.

Source: School Leavers' Survey, 1997/8 leavers.

In keeping with previous research, males are found to have higher drop-out rates at junior cycle than females (Table 5.2). Students from professional and non-manual backgrounds have lower drop-out rates than those from other social classes. Furthermore, drop-out rates are significantly higher among students from households where neither parent is employed than among those from other household types (Table 5.2). Region is taken into account because previous research has indicated regional differences in educational participation with higher participation evident in Western areas (see, for example, Clancy, 2001). Junior cycle drop-out did not vary significantly by region, although rates of early school leaving were somewhat lower in the West and South-West. Controlling for social background along with region, the small minority (5 per cent) of students who work part-time while in first year are found to be almost two and a half times more likely than non-working students to drop out of school before the Junior Certificate.

Using the Schools Database, analyses were carried out to explore the association between working part-time during the Junior Cert year and subsequent drop-out from school (see Table 5.3). Differentiation in drop-out rates by gender, social class and parental employment is broadly consistent with the pattern found at junior cycle level. Thus, drop-out rates are higher among males, those from working-class backgrounds, and those from households where neither parent is in paid employment. Contrary to the pattern at junior cycle, there is significant regional variation in senior cycle drop-out rates with somewhat higher levels found in the East, North-East and Mid-West. As might be expected, students who obtained higher Junior Cert exam grades are less likely to drop out of school in the course of the senior cycle.

All else being equal, drop-out rates are found to be 1.4 times higher among students who had a part-time job in their Junior Cert year than among non-working students (Table 5.3, Model 1), a difference that is only partly accounted for by lower exam grades among working students (Table 5.3, Model 2).

Table 5.3: Part-time work and senior cycle drop-out

	Model 1	**Model 2**	**Model 3**	**Model 4**
Constant	0.150	1.939***	0.143	1.923***
Male	0.708***	0.359***	0.668***	0.338***
Parental class:				
Higher prof.	−0.407**	0.112	−0.413**	0.099
Lower prof.	−0.297*	0.009	−0.297*	0.005
Other non-manual	−0.520***	−0.326*	−0.524***	−0.335*
Skilled manual	−0.095	−0.030	−0.096	−0.034
(Base: Semi/unskilled manual)				
Parental employment:				
Neither employed	0.534***	0.350**	0.544***	0.358**
Both employed	−0.161	−0.110	−0.151	−0.103
(Base: One employed)				
Region of school:				
East	0.384*	0.199	0.404*	0.216
North-East	0.476*	0.454*	0.486*	0.462*
North-West	−0.041	0.049	−0.038	0.055
Midlands	0.025	0.031	0.038	0.038
Mid-West	0.516*	0.456*	0.512*	0.452
South-West	0.109	0.251	0.113	0.251
South-East	0.379	0.287	0.368	0.277
(Base: West)				
Ability test score	−0.057***	0.002	−0.057***	0.003
Part-time work:				
Worked part-time	0.314***	0.238***		
Hours worked:				
<10 hours			0.070	0.097
11-15 hours			0.448*	0.222
16-20 hours			0.762***	0.591*
>20 hours			0.972***	0.699**
(Base: Did not work)				
Junior Cert grade point average		−0.708***		−0.705***
N	*5466*	*5417*	*5466*	*5417*
Pseudo R²	*0.224*	*0.362*	*0.229*	*0.364*

Note: *** p<.001, ** p<.01, * p<.05; dummy variables have been included for missing data but are not reported. *Source*: Schools Database, 1994.

On closer inspection, the relationship between part-time work and school drop-out is found to vary by the number of hours worked. In Figure 5.5, the first series of columns indicates the predicted odds ratio of dropping out among working students compared to non-working students, controlling for gender, family background, region and prior ability. The second series of columns indicates the differences between working and non-working students adding in a further control for Junior Cert exam performance. Students working fewer than 10 hours per week do not differ significantly from those not in employment in their drop-out rates. Those working 11 to 15 hours are 1.6 times more likely to drop out than those not working while the relevant ratios are 2.1 for those working 16 to 20 hours and 2.6 for those working more than 20 hours per week. When Junior Cert performance is taken into account, the effect of working 11 to 15 hours is no longer significant, that is, students in this group are more likely to drop out because they tend to under-perform in their exam but, once this is taken into account, they are not at a higher risk than other students. Even controlling for Junior Cert grades, however, those working more than 15 hours per week are at a significantly higher risk of dropping out of school.

Figure 5.5: Drop-out pattern by employment and hours of work, comparing workers and non-workers

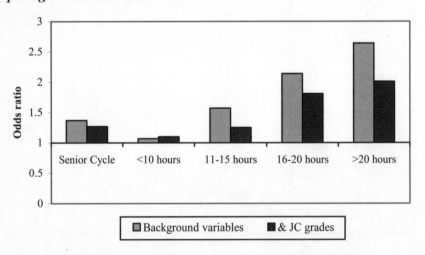

Note: Derived from models in Table 5.3. A ratio of 1 indicates no difference.
Source: Schools Database, 1994.

Separate analyses were carried out for males and females in order to explore the potential association between part-time work and school drop-out (analyses not shown here). Among males, even those working fewer than ten hours are at a higher risk of drop-out than students who are not working. In contrast, only females working more than 15 hours per week experience a higher drop-out risk.

The differences in drop-out rates between working and non-working students may be due not only to differences in their background characteristics but also to underlying differences in their orientation to school life. Table 5.4 explores the relationship between student attitudes to school prior to the Junior Cert exam and their tendency to drop out of school at senior cycle level. The definitions of the variables used to measure student attitudes are detailed in Appendix 5.1. Students who have experienced more negative interaction with teachers at junior cycle are more likely to drop out of school (Model 1, Table 5.4). Conversely, students who view their school life as happy (at junior cycle level) are less likely to drop out as are those who have more positive views of their own abilities (over and above their actual ability levels). As might be expected, educational aspirations at age 14 are highly predictive of subsequent behaviour regarding participation in education. Students with poor attendance records in their Junior Cert year are over twice as likely as those with average/good records to drop out of school after the end of the year.

The influences of student–teacher interaction and academic self-image are mediated through Junior Cert performance; that is, students who experience negative interaction with teachers and have negative views of their own abilities are more likely to drop out of school because they under-perform in their Junior Cert exam (Model 2, Table 5.4). Students who are less satisfied with school, who have low aspirations and a poor attendance record are more likely to drop out of school, even when their educational performance is taken into account. Even controlling for student attitudes and Junior Cert performance, those who worked part-time in their Junior Cert year are found to have higher drop-out rates than their non-working counterparts so working part-time does appear to be associated with a greater tendency to leave school early. This is consistent with some research from the United States and Australia which indicates that part-time employment tends to draw students away from their studies and leads to increased school drop-out (see Robinson, 1999; Marsh, 1991).

Table 5.4: Student attitudes, part-time work and senior cycle drop-out

	Model 1	**Model 2**
Constant	1.382***	2.264***
Female	−0.425***	−0.229*
Social class:		
Higher professional	−0.002	0.251
Lower professional	−0.075	0.095
Other non-manual	−0.398**	−0.300*
Skilled manual	−0.054	−0.023
(Base: Semi/unskilled manual)		
Parental employment:		
Neither employed	0.357*	0.279*
Both employed	−0.103	−0.072
(Base: One parent employed)		
Ability test score	−0.034***	0.006
Part-time work in Junior Cert year	0.206*	0.187†
Attitudes to schooling (in JC year):		
Positive teacher interaction	0.199*	0.117
Negative teacher interaction	0.270***	0.126
School satisfaction	−0.142**	−0.125*
Academic self-image	−0.233*	0.009
Educational aspirations	−0.746***	−0.519***
Poor attendance record	0.825***	0.608***
(Base: Good attendance)		
Junior Cert performance		−0.567***
N	*5466*	*5417*
Pseudo R²	*0.342*	*0.400*

Note: *** $p<.001$, ** $p<.01$, * $p<.05$, † $p<.10$.

Source: Schools Database, 1994.

5.3: EXAMINATION PERFORMANCE

The Schools Database allows us to control for a range of student characteristics in exploring the relationship between part-time work and examination performance at both Junior and Leaving Cert levels. For Junior Cert grades, points were allocated to each grade achieved (ranging from 0 to 10) and averaged over all exam subjects taken to produce an overall measure of performance (see Appendix 5.1). An ordinary least squares regression model was used to predict the effect of a range of factors on Junior Cert performance. Positive coefficients indicate the factor is associated with higher Junior Cert grades; negative coefficients indicate the variable is related to lower grades.

In keeping with previous research (see, for example, Hannan et al., 1996), exam grades at Junior Cert level are found to be higher among girls, students from professional backgrounds and those with higher prior ability levels (see Table 5.5). Students who work part-time are found to achieve significantly lower exam grades, on average, than those who do not work. Figure 5.6 indicates the scale of the Junior Cert performance differences between working and non-working students, controlling for background factors. Students who work fewer than ten hours resemble those without paid work in their average grades. However, students who work more than ten hours per week do significantly worse than non-working students with the lowest grades found among those working more than twenty hours per week.

Table 5.5: Part-time work and exam performance

	Junior Cert	
	Model 1	*Model 2*
Constant	3.052	3.031
Male	−0.652***	−0.628***
Parental class:		
Higher professional	0.831***	0.844***
Lower professional	0.603***	0.619***
Other non-manual	0.432***	0.456***
Skilled manual	0.182**	0.193***
(Base: Semi/unskilled manual)		
Parental employment:		
Neither employed	−0.306***	−0.310***
Both employed	0.030	0.034
(Base: One employed)		
Region of school:		
East	−0.308***	−0.291***
North-East	−0.152	−0.156
North-West	−0.089	−0.073
Midlands	0.008	−0.010
Mid-West	−0.236**	−0.219*
South-West	0.170*	0.173*
South-East	−0.246**	−0.217*
(Base: West)		
Ability test score	0.080***	0.079***
JC grade point average		
Part-time work:		
Worked part-time	−0.183***	
Hours worked:		
<10 hours		−0.009
11–15 hours		−0.427***
16–20 hours		−0.450***
>20 hours		−0.603***
(Base: Did not work)		
N	*5678*	*5641*
Adjusted R²	*0.557*	*0.561*

Note: *** p<.001, ** p<.01, * p<.05.
Source: Schools Database, 1994.

Figure 5.6: Junior Cert exam grades among working students compared with non-working students

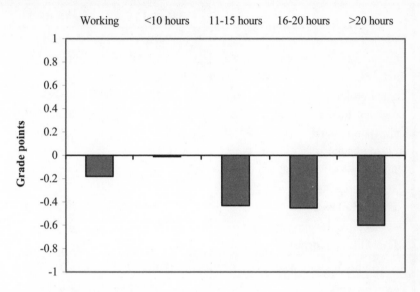

Note: Derived from Table 5.5.

Source: Schools Database, 1994.

However, as indicated in Chapter 2, students who work part-time differ from their non-working counterparts in terms of their overall orientation to schooling. Table 5.6 considers the relationship between part-time work and Junior Cert exam performance, controlling for attitudes to schooling. Students who have experienced negative feedback from teachers tend to under-perform in their exams relative to their initial ability levels. Furthermore, students with poor attendance records tend to achieve lower grades than their counterparts with average or good attendance levels. Those with a more positive view of their own abilities tend to achieve higher grades as do those who intend to stay on in full-time education.

Table 5.6: *Student attitudes, part-time work and Junior Cert exam performance*

	Model 1	Model 2
Constant	2.012	1.964
Female	0.463***	0.445***
Social class:		
Higher professional	0.484***	0.493***
Lower professional	0.377***	0.398***
Other non-manual	0.318***	0.330***
Skilled manual	0.114*	0.123*
(Base: Semi-skilled manual)		
Parental employment:		
Neither employed	−0.251***	−0.244***
Both employed	−0.009	0.003
(Base: One employed)		
Prior ability/performance	0.063***	0.062***
Part-time work	−0.041	
Hours of work:		
<10 hours		0.077
Over 10 hours		−0.237***
(Base: Did not work)		
Attitudes to schooling:		
Positive teacher interaction	−0.106***	−0.113***
Negative teacher interaction	−0.315***	−0.313***
School satisfaction	0.050*	0.049*
Academic self-image	0.321***	0.345***
Educational aspirations	0.468***	0.469***
Poor attendance record	−0.468***	−0.475***
(Base: Good attendance)		
N	*5678*	*5678*
Adjusted R²	*0.667*	*0.667*

Note: *** $p<.001$, ** $p<.01$, * $p<.05$.

Source: Schools Database, 1994.

When student orientations to school are taken into account, part-time work per se no longer has a significant association with Junior Cert performance (Table 5.6, Model 1). This is because the effect of part-time work on performance is mediated through educational aspirations; in other words, working students tend to do worse in the Junior Cert chiefly because they have lower educational aspirations. It may be that students' aspirations have been negatively affected by working part-time. Unfortunately, the causal relationship cannot be disentangled without longitudinal data in which measures of student attitudes before they started to work are available. However, it is worth noting that those working over 10 hours a week still under-perform relative to other students when their attitudes to school are taken into account (Table 5.6, Model 2).

Table 5.7 presents a model predicting Leaving Cert performance. Models 1 and 3 examine the impact of a range of factors on Leaving Cert *performance* overall while the control for Junior Cert performance in models 2 and 4 means that these models estimate the impact of the specified factors on *progress* in the Leaving Certificate relative to how students performed in the Junior Cert. Girls and students from professional backgrounds do better overall and make more progress over the senior cycle. Figure 5.7 presents the predicted performance gap between working and non-working students; the first set of columns control for gender, social background and region while the second set of columns include an additional control for Junior Cert performance. Students who work part-time in their Leaving Cert year achieve significantly lower grades overall and the performance gap increases with number of hours worked (see Models 1 and 3, Table 5.7 and the first set of columns in Figure 5.7). However, students who work in their Leaving Cert year also differ from non-working students in their Junior Cert performance.

Table 5.7: Part-time work and Leaving Cert exam performance

	Model 1	Model 2	Model 3	Model 4
Constant	7.500	−5.738	7.450	−5.726
Male	−0.809***	−0.177*	−0.691***	−0.155*
Parental class:				
Higher professional	3.179***	0.767***	3.164***	0.767***
Lower professional	2.248***	0.563***	2.189***	0.542***
Other non-manual	1.193***	0.146	1.135***	0.147
Skilled manual	0.158	−0.036	0.153	−0.045
(Base: Semi/ unskilled manual)				
Parental employment:				
Neither employed	−0.780***	−0.101	−0.762***	−0.106
Both employed	0.245	−0.077	0.255*	−0.087
(Base: One empld)				
Region of school:				
East	−0.329	0.259	−0.400	0.257
North-East	−0.329	−0.540**	−0.414	−0.550**
North-West	−0.212	−0.166	−0.196	−0.164
Midlands	−0.450	−0.217	−0.503	−0.219
Mid-West	−0.362	0.011	−0.354	0.059
South-West	0.413	0.139	0.457*	0.171
South-East	−0.421	0.020	−0.514	−0.008
(Base: West)				
Part-time work:				
Worked part-time	−1.481***	−0.577***		
Hours worked:				
≤ 10 hours			−0.969***	−0.456***
11–15 hours			−1.619***	−0.602***
16–20 hours			−2.395***	−0.900***
>20 hours			−3.112***	−0.834**
(Base: Did not work)				
Junior Cert grade point average		1.988***		1.985***
N	*4663*	*4431*	*4663*	*4431*
Adjusted R^2	*0.141*	*0.675*	*0.148*	*0.676*

Note: *** $p<.001$, ** $p<.01$, * $p<.05$. *Source*: Schools Database, 1994.

Figure 5.7: Leaving Cert exam grades among working students

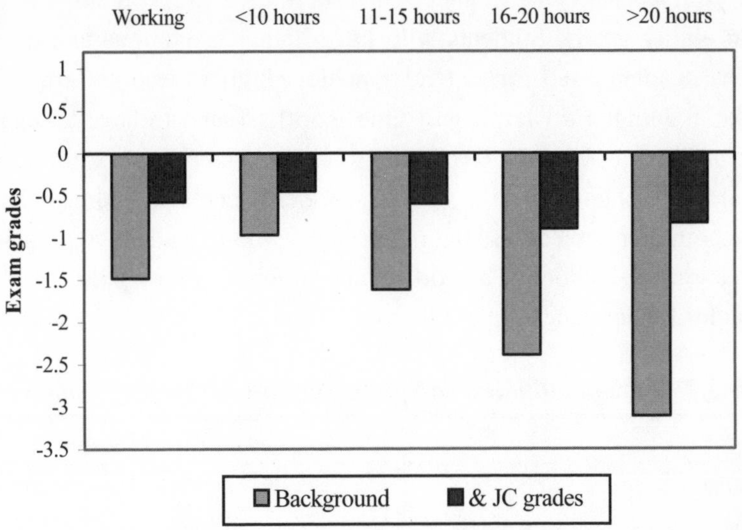

Note: Derived from models in Table 5.7. *Source*: Schools Database, 1994.

Controlling for Junior Cert grades, working students are found to achieve significantly lower exam grades, by 0.6 grade points on average per subject, than those who do not work. Contrary to the pattern at Junior Cert level, even those working fewer than ten hours per week appear to achieve lower grades than those not at work (see Figure 5.7). However, it should be noted that this may actually represent an underestimate of the effect of part-time work if students in part-time work at senior cycle also worked prior to the Junior Cert. If a student works prior to the Junior Cert and this negatively affects Junior Cert performance, controlling for Junior Cert grades may mask the full negative effects of part-time work on Leaving Cert performance. As a result, the estimated performance gap of 0.6 grade points per subject can be taken to represent a conservative estimate of the difference between working and non-working students at Leaving Cert level. The estimated performance gap is roughly equivalent to 18 CAO points.

Furthermore, as indicated in Chapter 2, students who work part-time differ from their non-working counterparts in terms of their overall orientation to schooling. Table 5.8 considers the relationship between part-time work and exam performance, controlling for attitudes to schooling.

As at Junior Cert level, students who have experienced negative feedback from teachers tend to under-perform in their exams relative to their initial ability levels. Students who have higher aspirations and a more positive academic self-image tend to achieve higher Leaving Cert grades. Unlike at Junior Cert level, part-time work is found to have a negative relationship with Leaving Cert exam grades, even controlling for student attitudes to schooling, with working students achieving almost half a grade point per subject less than their non-working students with similar orientations to school. This difference amounts to roughly 14 CAO points for higher education entry.

Table 5.8: Student attitudes, part-time work and exam performance

	Leaving Cert Grades
Constant	−7.072
Female	0.142*
Social class:	
Higher professional	0.631***
Lower professional	0.441***
Other non-manual	0.060
Skilled manual	−0.041
(Base: Semi/unskilled manual)	
Parental employment:	
Neither employed	−0.081
Both employed	−0.116
(Base: One employed)	
Junior Cert performance	1.610***
Part-time work	−0.474***
Attitudes to schooling:	
Positive teacher interaction	−0.110
Negative teacher interaction	−0.631***
School satisfaction	0.063
Academic self-image	0.711***
Educational aspirations	1.040***
N	*4431*
Adjusted R^2	*0.713*

Note: *** $p<.001$, ** $p<.01$, * $p<.05$. *Source*: Schools Database, 1994.

In sum, working part-time is associated with underperformance at both Junior and Leaving Cert levels. At Junior Cert level, the pattern is mainly due to lower educational aspirations among working students. It may be that these students are disengaged from school life and seek paid employment as an alternative form of self-fulfilment. Even so, Junior Cert students who work more than ten hours a week remain at a disadvantage in performance terms. At Leaving Cert level, the pattern is more clear-cut. Regardless of the number of hours students work and their attitudes to school, working students achieve lower grades than non-working students. This pattern is likely to reflect the greater number of hours of study required for Leaving Cert exam success. Our findings lend support to the zero sum model discussed in Chapter 1 whereby part-time employment, particularly that involving long hours, reduces the amount of time available for schoolwork and leads to underperformance among students.

5.4: OUT-OF-SCHOOL ACTIVITIES

Part-time work is potentially only one out-of-school activity which may mitigate against student academic achievement. High levels of involvement in household labour, sports, watching television and other social activities may also adversely affect exam grades.

Figure 5.8: Difference in exam performance between non-working and working students at different levels of involvement in social activities

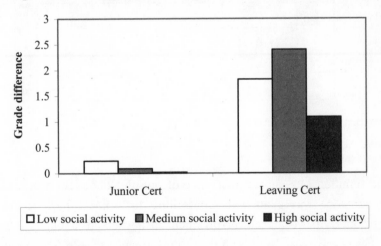

Source: Schools Database, 1994.

Chapter 3 indicated the role of part-time work in funding a more active social life among second-level students. For the purposes of this analysis, involvement in social activities relates to the frequency of going to a disco, concert or cinema, going out on a date or taking alcohol with friends (see Appendix 5.1). Figure 5.8 shows the performance gap between non-working and working students at various levels of involvement in social activities. At Junior Cert level, working is associated with under-performance among students with a low level of involvement in social activities. However, there is no difference in performance between workers and non-workers when they have a very active social life. At Leaving Cert level, workers under-perform relative to non-workers regardless of their level of involvement in social activities. However, the gap in performance between workers and non-workers is greater for those with less active social lives.

Figure 5.9: *Leaving Cert exam performance, part-time work and involvement in out-of-school activities*

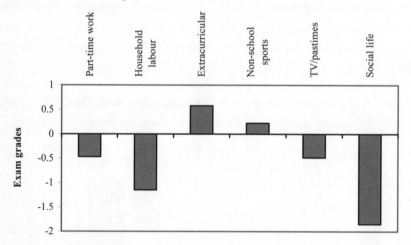

Note: Derived from Table 5.9.

Source: Schools Database, 1994.

The simultaneous impact of a range of out-of-school activities on exam performance was examined. Controlling for student background and prior ability/performance, involvement in household labour is found to be negatively associated with exam performance (Table 5.9). Participation in extra-curricular activities is not significantly related to performance at Junior Cert level but is positively associated with Leaving Cert exam grades. This pattern may be related to a greater sense of involvement in school life generally among these students with consequent benefits for their academic engagement within school (see Smyth, 1999). In contrast, participation in (non-school) sports is positively associated with Junior Cert performance but has no significant relationship with Leaving Cert performance, once Junior Cert grades have been taken into account. Students who have a more active social life achieve lower exam grades as do those who spend longer watching television (or engaging in other pastimes). Figure 5.9 indicates the scale of the Leaving Cert performance difference for those with high levels of involvement in the various activities compared with working part-time.[3]

As indicated by Table 5.9, participation in part-time work per se is not significantly related to Junior Cert exam performance, once other out-of-school activities are taken into account. This occurs because of the strong relationship between having a part-time job and having a more active social life. If part-time work has a negative "effect" on Junior Cert performance, it is because students who work part-time at this stage have already to some extent "withdrawn" from school to become involved in employment and social activities and these social activities are further facilitated by their income from employment. This contrasts with the pattern at Leaving Cert level where part-time work is negatively associated with exam grades, regardless of the level of involvement in other out-of-school activities.[4]

---

[3] The criteria for high involvement in the various activities are specified in Appendix 5.1.

[4] A propensity score analysis matching students with different levels of involvement in social activities, background characteristics and attitudes to school also indicated a performance gap between working and non-working students (see Appendix 5.2).

Table 5.9: Out-of-school activities and exam performance

	Junior Cert	Leaving Cert
Constant	4.109	−3.169
Female	0.624***	0.258***
Social class:		
Higher professional	0.643***	0.822***
Lower professional	0.521***	0.549***
Other non-manual	0.364***	0.148
Skilled manual	0.143**	−0.050
(Base: Semi/unskilled manual)		
Parental employment:		
Neither employed	−0.309***	−0.117
Both employed	0.014	−0.009
(Base: One employed)		
Prior ability/performance	0.073***	1.873***
Part-time work	−0.034	−0.470***
Out-of-school activities:		
Household labour	−0.145***	−0.382***
Extra-curricular activities	−0.004	0.144***
Sports (non-school)	0.139***	0.074
Time on TV and other pastimes	−0.164***	−0.162***
Social life	−0.197***	−0.231***
N	*5678*	*4431*
Adjusted R^2	*0.623*	*0.688*

Note: *** $p<.001$, ** $p<.01$, * $p<.05$.

Source: Schools Database, 1994.

5.5: LABOUR MARKET INTEGRATION

The Annual School Leavers' Survey allows us to explore the association between part-time employment at school and measures of post-school activity, including participation in further education, unemployment levels, entry to apprenticeship, pay levels and type of occupation.

Table 5.10: Participation in post-school education (one year after leaving school)

	Model 1	Model 2	Model 3	Model 4
Constant	−0.083	−3.493***	−0.083	−3.480***
Worked part-time while at school	−0.446***	−0.292*		
Hours worked weekly:				
< 10 Hours			−0.130	−0.208
11–15 Hours			−0.649***	−0.251
16–20 Hours			−0.528***	−0.194
> 20 Hours			−0.839***	−0.755**
Background characteristics:				
Male		−0.315*		−0.308*
Parental Social Class:				
Higher prof.		1.019***		1.017***
Lower prof.		0.521*		0.484*
Other non-manual		0.390		0.374
Skilled manual		0.097		0.099
(Base: semi/unskilled manual)				
Parental Employment:				
Neither Employed		−0.564*		−0.600*
Both Employed		−0.015		−0.032
(Base: one parent employed)				
Region while at School:				
East		−0.753**		−0.755**
North-East		0.732*		0.716*
North-West		−0.258		−0.270
Midland		0.511		0.517
Mid-West		−0.588		−0.579
South-West		−0.564		−0.622*
South-East		−0.006		0.008
(Base: West)				
Educational Attainment:				
Junior Cert		1.422		1.429
Leaving Cert Fail		3.525***		3.550***
Leaving Cert Pass		2.397*		2.408*
Leaving Cert 1-3 hons		3.911***		3.917***
Leaving Cert 4+ hons		5.532***		5.541***
(Base: Unqualified)				
N	*2498*	*1410*	*2497*	*1409*
Pseudo R²	*0.016*	*0.480*	*0.027*	*0.484*

Note: *** p<.001, ** p<.01, * p<.05. *Source*: 1997/8 School Leavers' Survey.

5.5.1: Access to further education

Table 5.10 examines the relationship between a range of background variables and being in full-time education/training one year after leaving school. In overall terms, those who worked part-time while at school are significantly less likely (0.6 times as likely) than non-workers to go on to further education (see Model 1). Young men are less likely than similarly qualified young women to be in full-time education or training one year after leaving school. In keeping with previous research, post-school educational participation levels are highest among those from higher professional backgrounds, even controlling for their exam performance. There is some regional variation in participation levels, with the highest levels found in the North-East and the West and the lowest levels found in the East, all else being equal. As might be expected, attaining four or more higher-level grades in the Leaving Certificate is strongly predictive of entry to further study.

Controlling for background factors and educational attainment, post-school educational participation is found to be significantly lower among those who engaged in part-time work while at school. The effect of employment on the likelihood of engaging in further study is partially mediated through educational attainment; in other words, part-time workers are less likely to go on to further education partly because of their lower educational qualifications. However, at the same level of educational attainment, working students are less likely to pursue further studies than non-working students (Model 2, Table 5.10).

When the number of hours worked is examined, those who work fewer than ten hours per week are found to resemble non-workers in terms of their post-school educational levels (Model 3, Table 5.10). The lower levels of participation among those working ten to twenty hours a week are primarily due to the fact that working has a negative influence on educational attainment and hence on post-school study (see Model 4, Table 5.10). However, even controlling for educational performance, those who worked more than twenty hours a week are less than half as likely as non-working students to go on to further education. In the case of these young people, a heavy investment in part-time work appears to channel them away from post-school study, a pattern which is consistent with previous research in the United States (see, for example, Marsh, 1991).

5.5.2: Access to employment

While those who work have a lower probability of pursuing further study and a greater probability of entering the labour market upon leaving school, part-time work may have benefits in terms of smoothing the transition into full-time employment. Table 5.11 examines the probability of being unemployed (rather than employed) one year after leaving school. Eleven per cent of the sample were unemployed one year after leaving school. Those who worked part-time while at school have lower unemployment levels, both overall and controlling for background and educational characteristics. Young men are found to have lower unemployment levels than young women, controlling for educational attainment. There is no significant variation in unemployment chances by parental social class or region when educational level is taken into account. However, there is a slight tendency towards higher unemployment among young people from households where neither parent was employed. This may reflect less access to employment networks among these young people or alternatively it may reflect higher levels of unemployment within the local labour market. Unemployment levels are somewhat lower across all levels of employment intensity, although the greatest advantage in terms of avoiding unemployment appears to accrue to those who worked 16 to 20 hours per week (Model 4, Table 5.11). Further analysis was conducted to explore the relationship between having worked in the most recent school year and unemployment chances (analyses not shown here). The pattern for having worked in the most recent year at school resembles that for having worked at any point in the school career, with lower unemployment chances among those who had worked.

Table 5.11: Probability of being unemployed versus employed one year after leaving school (among those who entered the labour market)

	Model 1	Model 2	Model 3	Model 4
Constant	−1.650***	−0.040	−1.650***	−0.105
Worked part-time while at school	−1.026***	−0.722*		
Hours Worked Weekly				
< 10 Hours			−1.193***	−0.568
11–15 Hours			−0.638*	−0.439
16–20 Hours			−1.455***	−1.644***
> 20 Hours			−0.783*	−0.280
Background Chars.:				
Male		−0.592*		−0.565*
Parental Social Class:				
Higher Professional		−0.707		−0.725
Lower Professional		0.137		0.189
Other non-manual		−0.384		−0.294
Skilled manual		−0.091		−0.069
(Base: semi/unskilled manual)				
Parental Employment:				
Neither Employed		0.677		0.752*
Both Employed		−0.442		−0.427
(Base: one parent employed)				
Region While at School:				
East		−0.051		−0.035
North-East		−0.116		−0.152
North-West		0.110		0.114
Midland		0.033		0.039
Mid-West		−0.322		−0.325
South-West		−2.059		−2.047
South-East		0.529		0.546
(Base: West)				
Educational Attainment:				
Junior Cert		−1.282***		−1.305***
Leaving Cert Fail		−0.615		−0.581
Leaving Cert Pass		−2.233***		−2.205***
Leaving Cert 1-3 hons		−1.505***		−1.520***
Leaving Cert 4+ hons		−2.560***		−2.557**
(Base: Unqualified)				
N	*1673*	*888*	*1673*	*888*
Pseudo R²	*0.048*	*0.203*	*0.054*	*0.216*

Note: *** p<.001, ** p<.01, * p<.05. *Source*: 1997/8 School Leavers' Survey.

Overall, it appears that part-time work experience while at school does have the effect of reducing the probability of unemployment. Whether such early labour market experience operates to improve job search skills, promote labour market adaptability, promote the skills associated with successful employment or provide direct linkages with employers, it is not possible to say on the basis of available data. Early labour market exposure (while at school) does appear to increase the chances of a smooth transition into the labour market after leaving school. However, it should be noted that these analyses only capture short-term effects since they relate solely to young people who go into the labour market directly after leaving school. Their chances of employment in the longer term may still not be as advantageous as those of their counterparts who went on to third-level education.

5.5.3: Access to apprenticeships

It may be that by working part-time, young people develop links with employers and go on to enter an apprenticeship. Entry to apprenticeship is highly gendered with young men being more than 14 times as likely as equally qualified young women to become apprentices (Table 5.12). Apprentices are disproportionately drawn from those with a Junior Certificate, a "pass" Leaving Certificate or those with fewer than three higher-level Leaving Cert subjects. In overall terms, those who work part-time at school are somewhat less likely than non-workers to go on to an apprenticeship (see Model 1, Table 5.12). However, these differences are related to the differing profiles of workers and non-workers with no significant differences apparent once background and educational characteristics are taken into account (Model 2, Table 5.12).

Table 5.12: Probability of being in apprenticeship one year after leaving school (among those who entered the labour market)

	Model 1	Model 2	Model 3	Model 4
Constant	−1.475***	−5.147***	−1.475***	−5.199***
Worked part-time while at school	−0.337*	−0.146		
Hours Worked Weekly				
< 10 Hours			−0.318	−0.067
11–15 Hours			−0.511	−0.678
16–20 Hours			−0.349	−0.089
> 20 Hours			−0.182	−0.023
Background characteristics				
Male		2.607***		2.606***
Parental Social Class:				
Higher Professional		0.442		0.409
Lower Professional		−0.005		−0.004
Other non-manual		0.591		0.616
Skilled manual		0.369		0.371
(Base: semi/unskilled manual)				
Parental Employment:				
Neither Employed		−0.740		−0.697
Both Employed		0.098		0.122
(Base: one parent employed)				
Region While at School:				
East		−0.573		−0.515
North-East		−0.121		−0.064
North-West		−0.617		−0.584
Midland		−0.478		−0.477
Mid-West		−0.439		−0.418
South-West		−0.524		−0.497
South-East		−0.367		−0.373
(Base: West)				
Educational Attainment:				
Junior Cert		2.358**		2.369***
Leaving Cert Fail		−0.130		−0.168
Leaving Cert Pass		2.392***		2.392**
Leaving Cert 1–3 hons		1.570*		1.597*
Leaving Cert 4+ hons		0.653		0.671
(Base: Unqualified)				
N	1670	886	1670	886
Pseudo R^2	0.007	0.308	0.008	0.311

Note: *** $p<.001$, ** $p<.01$, * $p<.05$. *Source*: 1997/8 School Leavers' Survey.

5.5.4: Quality of employment

Log hourly pay was examined among young people whose principal activity was employment (Table 5.13). Pay levels were moderately but significantly higher among those who had worked while at school, even controlling for other characteristics. Further analysis (not shown here) indicated that having worked in the last year at school had a somewhat stronger relationship with current pay than having any work experience while at school. It should be noted that the pay differences between working and non-working students entering the labour market, while significant, are comparatively modest and pay levels among this group are likely to be markedly lower than among those who will graduate with third-level qualifications.

Contrary to previous research (see, for example, Breen et al., 1995), there was little variation by educational attainment or region in overall pay levels. Overall, the model explains little of the variation in pay levels among the school leavers studied. However, it should be noted that information on pay levels was missing for almost half of those in paid employment.

Table 5.14 examines the factors which are associated with entry into clerical and service as opposed to manual occupations. Because of the lack of significant regional variation, region while at school is not included in these models. In addition, because of the small number of those without qualifications in paid employment, those with no qualifications and those with a Junior Cert are grouped together. Patterns of occupational entry are highly gendered, with young men markedly less likely to enter clerical or service jobs than similarly qualified young women. Young people from a higher professional background are more likely to enter clerical jobs, even controlling for their educational background. Having any kind of Leaving Cert qualification is associated with entry into a clerical job, although having four or more higher level grades has a stronger association with clerical entry. Controlling for background and qualifications, those who worked part-time while at school are more likely to enter clerical or service jobs than their non-working counterparts. This may relate to the concentration of working students in white-collar jobs (see Chapter 4). The pattern may also help to explain the pay differentials between working and non-working students indicated above.

Table 5.13: Hourly pay (log) among those whose principal activity was employment

	Model 1	Model 2	Model 3	Model 4
Constant	1.535	1.520	1.535	1.517
Worked part-time while at school	0.068**	0.067*		
Hours Worked Weekly				
< 10 Hours			0.065†	0.071
11-15 Hours			0.092*	0.055
16-20 Hours			0.068†	0.068
>20 Hours			0.044	0.072
Background characteristics				
Male		−0.044		−0.043
Parental Social Class:				
Higher Professional		−0.021		−0.021
Lower Professional		0.058		0.058
Other non-manual		−0.013		−0.012
Skilled manual		−0.009		−0.008
(Base: semi/ unskilled manual)				
Parental Employment:				
Neither Employed		0.085		0.086
Both Employed		0.014		0.014†
(Base: one parent employed)				
Region While at School:				
East		0.031		0.034
North-East		−0.098		−0.097
North-West		−0.141		−0.139
Midland		−0.019		−0.019
Mid-West		−0.154†		−0.152†
South-West		−0.082		−0.079
South-East		−0.077		−0.077
(Base: West)				
Educational Attainment:				
Junior Cert		0.054		0.054
Leaving Cert Fail		0.079		0.077
Leaving Cert Pass		−0.001		−0.001
Leaving Cert 1-3 hons		0.025		0.026
Leaving Cert 4+ hons		0.069		0.070
(Base: Unqualified)				
N		*682*	*398*	*682*
Pseudo R²	*0.01*	*0.048*	*0.007*	*0.040*

Note: *** p<.001, ** p<.01, * p<.05, † p<.10. *Source*: 1997/8 School Leavers' Survey.

Table 5.14: Type of occupation entered among those whose principal activity was employment (contrasted against manual work)

	Clerical Job		Service Job	
	Model 1	*Model 2*	*Model 1*	*Model 2*
Constant	−0.929***	−0.464	−0.672***	0.205
Worked part-time while at school	0.813*	0.397*	0.392**	0.329†
Background characteristics:				
Male		−2.111***		−1.603***
Parental Social Class:				
Higher Professional		0.801*		0.385
Lower Professional		0.304		0.092
Other non-manual		−0.107		−0.147
Skilled manual		−0.223		−0.086
(Base: semi/unskilled manual)				
Parental Employment:				
Neither Employed		−0.028		0.158
Both Employed		0.090		0.019
(Base: one parent employed)				
Educational Attainment:				
Leaving Cert Fail		1.161**		0.670†
Leaving Cert Pass		1.040***		0.030
Leaving Cert 1-3 hons		1.360***		0.122
Leaving Cert 4+ hons		1.573***		0.792*
(Base: Junior Cert or below)				
N	*1196*	*676*		
Pseudo R²	*0.030*	*0.273*		

Note: *** p<.001, ** p<.01, * p<.05, † p<.10. *Source*: 1997/8 School Leavers' Survey.

In sum, working part-time while at school appears to channel young people away from post-school education. However, at least in the short-term, it also appears to act as a protection against unemployment in their early labour market career, slightly enhances pay levels and facilitates access to white-collar employment. It should be noted that, in the longer term, young people who worked while at school may be at a disadvantage compared with their counterparts who went on to higher education.

5.6: CONCLUSIONS

This chapter has explored the relationship between part-time work while at school and a range of student outcomes, including school drop-out, exam performance and early labour market career. The analyses have allowed us to directly test whether the effects of part-time employment while at school on student outcomes are positive, negative or neutral.

Part-time employment is found to have a negative effect on educational participation and achievement. Students who worked while at school appear to be at greater risk of dropping out of school early. In addition, working students tend to under-perform in State examinations, although the pattern differs somewhat between Junior and Leaving Certificate levels. Among Junior Cert students, a high level of involvement (that is, working more than ten hours a week) is associated with lower grades in the Junior Cert exam. In large part, educational underperformance among Junior Cert students who work part-time is related to their higher level of involvement in out-of-school activities, particularly social activities, and lower educational aspirations. Unfortunately, without longitudinal data it is difficult to discern cause and effect. Do disengaged students who might be expected to achieve lower grades anyway become disproportionately involved in part-time work, or does work involvement itself facilitate a more active social life and hence less time spent on study? At Leaving Cert level, the pattern is more clear-cut. Regardless of the number of hours students work, their previous attitudes to school and their other out-of-school activities, working students achieve lower grades than non-working students. This pattern is likely to reflect the greater number of hours of study required for Leaving Cert exam success.

It is important to remember that part-time work is not the only out-of-school activity which may impact on student performance. High levels of student involvement in unpaid household labour are also associated with educational underperformance. Similarly, high levels of involvement in social activity tend to lead to lower exam grades. In contrast, participation in sports has a positive (or at worst, neutral) effect on exam grades.

Part-time work is not wholly negative in its effects, however. Students who have paid work experience before they leave school appear to make a smoother transition into the labour market. In the period immediately after leaving school, they are less likely to experience unemployment and, when employed, they receive moderately higher pay and are more likely to enter white-collar occupations than others in the labour market. These short-term benefits must, however, be balanced against the fact that working students are less likely to go on to further education which would yield a greatly improved quality of employment for participants in the longer term.

Appendix 5.1: Description of variables used in the analyses

Variables	Description
Outcomes	
Junior cycle drop-out	Dichotomous variable where 1=left school before the Junior Cert exam.
Senior cycle drop-out	Dichotomous variable where 1=left school before the Leaving Cert exam but after the Junior Cert exam.
Junior Cert performance	Points were allocated to each exam grade; the points ranged from 0 for E, F or NG grades to 10 for a higher level A grade. These points were averaged over all exam subjects taken.
Leaving Cert performance	Points were allocated to each exam grade; the points ranged from 0 for E, F or NG grades to 20 for a higher level A1 grade. These points were averaged over all exam subjects taken.
Post-school educational participation	Dummy variable where 1=in full-time education or training approximately one year after leaving school; contrasted against any other destination.
Unemployment	Dummy variable where 1=unemployed one year after leaving school; contrasted against being in employment.
Apprenticeship	Dummy variable where 1=in apprenticeship (either statutory or non-statutory) at the time of the survey; contrasted against any other labour market destination.
Hourly pay	Gross pay per hour worked in the previous week for those whose principal activity was employment; log value was taken.
Type of occupation: Clerical Service	Dummy variables where 1=in clerical or service work respectively at the time of the survey for those whose principal activity was employment; contrasted against being in a manual occupation.

Student Background	
Gender	Dummy variable where 1= female.
Social class: Higher prof. Lower prof. Non-manual Skilled manual	Census Social Class categories based on the occupational status of parents; contrasted against semi/unskilled manual workers.
Parental employment: Neither employed Both employed	Dummy variables where 1=neither parent is in employment or both parents are in employment respectively; contrasted against one parent in paid employment.
Region while at school	Set of dummy variables which indicate region while at school in the School Leavers' Survey and region within which school was located in the Schools Database; contrasted against located in the West.
Ability test score	VRNA, combined verbal reasoning and numerical ability scores.
Student attitudes	
Positive teacher interaction	Likert scale based on frequency of following items: (1) Have you been told that your work is good? (2) Have you been asked questions in class? (3) Have you been praised for answering a difficult question correctly? (4) Have you been praised because your written work is well done? Ranges from 1 (low) to 4 (high).
Negative teacher interaction	Likert scale based on frequency of following items: (1) Have you been given out to because your work is untidy or not done on time? (2) Have you wanted to ask or answer questions in class but were ignored? (3) Have you been given out to for misbehaving in class? (4) Teachers pay more attention in class to what some students say than to others. (5) I find most teachers hard to talk to. Values range from 1 (low) to 4 (high).
School satisfaction	Extent to which agrees with the statement that: 'For the most part, school life is a happy one for me'; values range from 1 (low) to 4 (high).

Academic Self-Image	Likert scale based on the following items: (1) I can do just about anything I set my mind to (2) I'm usually well ahead of others in my year in school (3) I am as good at school work as most other people my age (4) I'm hardly ever able to do what my teachers expect of me (reversed) (5) I'm usually well ahead of others in my class. Values range from 1 to 4.
Educational aspirations	Highest qualifications which the student expects to get; ranges from 1 (Junior Cert) to 4 (university degree).
Poor attendance record	Dummy variable where 1= pupil has poor/average attendance over the previous year; contrasted against good attendance.
Part-time work	
Part-time work (Schools Database)	Dummy variable where 1= pupil held a part-time job at time of interview; contrasted against those not working at time of interview.
Part-time work (School Leavers' Survey)	Dummy variable where 1=respondent engaged in any paid work during term-time while at school; contrasted against those who never worked while at school.
Hours worked	Set of dummy variables indicating worked fewer than 10 hours, 11 to 15 hours, 16 to 20 hours, over 20 hours; contrasted against not working.
Out of school activities	
Household labour	Likert scale based on involvement in the following tasks: • Making their bed • Swept the floor or vacuumed • Set the table for meals • Did the dishes or cleaned up after meals • Did any ironing • Put out the rubbish or cleaned up the yard. For the School Leavers' Survey, an additional item on frequency of looking after younger sisters or brothers was included. Values range from 1 (low) to 4 (high). High involvement is a score of 3 or more, that is, helped with each household task an average of 3 to 5 times in the previous two weeks.

Extra-curricular activities	Frequency of participation in school-organised sports and extracurricular activities (such as plays, debates etc.) in the previous two weeks. Values range from 2 (low) to 6 (high). High involvement is a score of 4 or more, that is, participated in each activity an average of 1 or 2 times in the previous two weeks.
Sports (non-school)	Frequency of participation in non-school sports over the previous two weeks. Values range from 1 (low) to 3 (high). High involvement is a score of 3, that is, participated in non-school sports 3 or more times in the previous two weeks.
Time on TV	Average number of hours per weeknight evening spent watching TV or on other pastimes. Values range from 0 to 8. High involvement is a score of 3 or more, that is, 3 hours per night spent watching TV or on pastimes.
Social life	Frequency of going to a disco, cinema or concert, taking alcohol with friends and going on a date in the previous two weeks. Values range from 3 (low) to 9 (high). High involvement is a score of 8 or more.

Appendix 5.2: Comparing working and non-working students using propensity score matching techniques

Propensity score matching techniques are designed to compare 'like with like' in examining the effect of a particular treatment on a specified outcome (see Conniffe et al., 2000). Since the relationship between part-time work and Junior Cert exam performance becomes insignificant when educational aspirations and/or social activity are entered into the model, the use of propensity score matching techniques is here limited to the Leaving Certificate sample.

Analyses using regression techniques have indicated a significant relationship between part-time work and Leaving Certificate performance, even controlling for student background, attitudes to school and involvement in other out-of-school activities. However, conventional regression techniques may overestimate the impact of group differences if the two groups are not well matched in terms of other characteristics. For example, if none of the non-working students had a high level of involvement in social activities, it would be hard to maintain that we were really comparing "like with like".

Two sets of analyses were conducted: the first relating to the impact of part-time work on Leaving Cert performance controlling for student background characteristics and attitudes to school; the second to the impact of part-time work on Leaving Cert performance controlling for background, school attitudes and involvement in out-of-school activities. Working students were found to differ from non-working students at Leaving Cert level in terms of their gender, social class background, Junior Cert performance, educational aspirations, academic self-image, participation in household labour, pastimes and social activities (see Chapters 2 and 5), all variables known to be associated with Leaving Cert performance.

For the first set of analyses, a propensity score was derived by using gender, parental social class, educational aspirations, negative student-teacher interaction, academic self-image and Junior Certificate performance (grade point average) to predict the probability of participation in part-time work among Leaving Cert students. The model which produced the best balance of covariates includes higher-order terms for Junior Cert grades and an interaction between gender and negative relations with teachers. The sample was initially divided into ten "bins" (or strata) of equal size on the basis of the propensity score. Two bins were found to be imbalanced in their propensity scores and were further subdivided yielding a total of twelve bins. Working and non-working students were found in all of the bins, with the proportion of working students ranging from 14 per cent in the lowest propensity bin to 44 per cent in the highest propensity bin. All of the covariates balanced within all of the bins, with the exception of somewhat lower academic self-image found among working students in bin 2. Average Leaving Cert performance by employment status was estimated within each bin. In ten of the twelve bins, working students had lower grades than non-workers. The weighted average difference between working and non-working students across the bins was 0.35 grades per exam subject. In addition, Leaving Cert performance was regressed on Junior Cert performance and working part-time within each bin. The coefficient for part-time work (averaged across all bins) was –0.3 compared with an unadjusted coefficient of –0.6 if a regression model is estimated on the basis of the whole sample. The adjusted regression coefficient of –0.3 is somewhat lower than that estimated using student background and attitudes to school as controls in a regression model (see Table 5.8 which gives an estimate of –0.47). However, it is clear that substantial differences in Leaving Cert performance remain between working and non-working students and that these differences are not due to measured differences in the background and attitudinal characteristics of the two groups.

A second set of analyses was conducted to explore whether performance differences between the two groups were due to their levels of involvement in out-of-school activities. A propensity score was estimated on the basis of the background and attitudinal variables used above along with levels of involvement in household roles, watching television and social activities. The sample was initially divided into ten "bins" with one bin subsequently subdivided to improve the balance of the covariates between working and non-working students. The covariates balanced within bins, with the exception of somewhat lower academic self-image among working students in bin 5, somewhat more negative relations among working students in bin 3 and a higher proportion of male students working in bin 9. In eight of the eleven bins, working students had lower average grades than non-working students. The average performance difference between working and non-working students across all bins was 0.2 grades per subject. Running separate regression models within bins yielded an average coefficient for part-time work across bins of –0.27. This provides a lower estimate of the Leaving Cert performance gap between workers and non-workers than that derived by including out-of-school activities in the regression model presented in Table 5.9 (which estimated the performance difference as –0.47 grade points).

In sum, comparing working students with non-working students with similar backgrounds, attitudes and levels of involvement in out-of-school activities provides a somewhat lower estimate of the performance gap between the two groups of students. However, all else being equal, students involved in paid work tend to under-perform at Leaving Cert level compared with those who do not engage in employment. As with the regression analysis, it should be noted that matching on Junior Cert performance may result in an underestimate of the effect of part-time work if students have also worked prior to the Junior Cert exam.

Chapter Six

SUMMARY AND CONCLUSIONS

6.1: CONTEXT OF THE STUDY

This study set out to examine the nature and effects of employment among second-level students in Ireland. Among the issues explored are the prevalence of student employment, the characteristics of those who work and do not work, the types of jobs in which students are employed, the commitments of their jobs in terms of hours and days worked, their motivations for working, the income and expenditure of students and the effects of their employment on a range of academic, social and labour market outcomes. The study draws on three main data sources: The Annual School Leavers' Surveys (conducted in 1999 and 2002), data developed from a national survey of students and schools conducted in 1994, and a survey of students in six schools with varying levels of student employment undertaken in late 2001. This chapter summarises some of the key findings of this research, identifies some implications for policy and points to issues for further study.

6.2: SUMMARY OF MAIN FINDINGS

6.2.1: Prevalence of part-time working

It is clear that paid employment among second-level students is now widespread, especially at senior cycle level. Over 60 per cent of Leaving Certificate students now have a regular part-time job. In addition, case-study evidence indicates that a significant proportion of female students engage in babysitting on an informal basis. The prevalence of employment entailing considerable hours during the school week is especially striking. In particular, male students are more likely to work longer hours and to engage in weekday work. Whether the changing economic climate will impact on these trends remains to be seen.

6.2.2: Characteristics of workers and non-workers

The influence of social background factors in employment rates shows some change over time. Most notably, social class and parental employment differentiation appear to become more marked over time. Students participating in more intensive work activities in the regular labour market are increasingly less likely to be from more economically advantaged backgrounds.

In terms of "subjective" attitudinal characteristics, some important differences between workers and non-workers are also apparent. Students engaged in employment are found to have lower educational aspirations and report higher levels of negative interaction with teachers. There is also some evidence that they are less likely to be happy with school generally, have more negative academic self-images and are likely to have poorer attendance records. However, it is not possible to identify the direction of causality: do less satisfied students select themselves into employment or does working part-time mean it is harder for students to cope with school life and its demands?

6.2.3: Nature of work

Concerning the nature and demands of the work in which students are engaged, school case-studies indicate that jobs are largely unskilled and unstructured in the sense that they are unrelated to school activities. Informal babysitting jobs are typically occupied by females and males are more likely to engage in more regular employment, occupying jobs which are typically more time-intensive. In addition, a significant minority, particularly of male students, are engaged in unpaid work, involving assistance on the family farm or in the family business.

Overall, males receive higher earnings for their employment, a disparity which is not solely explained by differences in the nature and regularity of the jobs males and females typically occupy. Within almost all types of job, males are rewarded with higher earnings. When income in the form of pocket money from parents is considered, again males are better off and, when total income is calculated, males are clearly in the advantageous position, a difference which holds when type of job and hours worked are considered.

6.2.4: Motivations for working/not working

A clear picture emerging from the case-studies of schools is the clear consumer orientation and motivation for students' working: part-time jobs are largely undertaken to finance a "lifestyle" rather than because of financial difficulty, to finance short-term consumption rather than to enhance human capital investments.

Among those not working a concern over school grades is a major factor in their decision, this being particularly notable among females and Leaving Cert students. In addition, the provision of financial support by parents is an important factor cited by students in allowing them not to work while at school.

A significant proportion of students consider that their parents and school do not approve of part-time employment. However, these views do not appear to play a major role in their employment decisions.

6.2.5: Effects of part-time work

International research on the impact of part-time work has centred on two explanatory models: the zero-sum model, which views employment as reducing available time for study and hence detracting from academic success, and the developmental model, which sees employment as contributing to the acquisition of a broader range of skills on the part of young people. Evidence from the Irish context lends some support to both frameworks but the negative effects of part-time employment would appear to outweigh the positive benefits for second-level students.

Part-time work while at school is associated with increased chances of early school leaving: those who work in first year are significantly more likely than their non-working counterparts to drop out of school before the Junior Certificate exam while those who work in their Junior Cert year are more likely to leave school before the end of secondary education. The risk of drop-out is especially evident among young people working more than fifteen hours a week.

On average, working students achieve lower exam grades than students not in paid employment. The pattern differs somewhat between Junior and Leaving Certificate levels. At Junior Cert level, educational underperformance among working students is partly due to the fact that students with low educational aspirations select themselves into employment and to the way in which part-time work facilitates a more active social life and hence less time spent on study. However, even taking these factors into account, working longer hours (more than ten hours a week) is related to lower Junior Cert exam grades. At Leaving Cert level, any level of involvement in paid work contributes to lower exam grades, with the greatest disadvantages accruing to those working longer hours. This is evident regardless of young people's long-term aspirations or their involvement in social activities outside school.

In spite of the negative effects of part-time work on retention and performance, there is some support for the view that employment contributes to the broader development of young people. Case-study evidence shows that young people tend to feel that their part-time work has enhanced their skills. National surveys of young people who have recently left full-time education indicate that part-time work while at school appears to smooth young people's transition into the labour market. At least in the short-term, having employment experience acts as a protection against unemployment and facilitates access to better-paying white-collar employment. Part-time work may, therefore, act as a "safety net" for young people who are not going on to higher education.

Much of the policy and research debate has centred on the effects, positive or negative, of part-time employment on academic and labour market outcomes among young people. However, paid part-time work is not the only activity that may reduce time spent on study. Students with high levels of involvement in unpaid household labour or in social activities are also found to under-perform in State examinations so it is important that part-time work should be seen in the context of out-of-school activities more generally.

6.3: ISSUES FOR FURTHER STUDY

This study has focussed on the relationship between employment while at school and the experiences of young people in their educational and early labour market careers. However, research conducted in the United States (see Ruhm, 1995) indicates that jobs held during school can yield substantial and lasting labour market benefits. Further research is needed to explore the longer-term economic attainment and labour market effects of student employment in the Irish context. It may be that by getting a "good start" in the labour market, young people who have worked while at school will have a secure career in the longer term. Conversely, it may be that these young people become 'locked into' the kind of low-skilled, service jobs which they held while at school and do not achieve significant career progression. Furthermore, given that young people who have worked while at school are less likely to access education or training immediately upon leaving school, it would be crucial to explore whether these young people return to education or training at a later point in their career.

6.4: CONCLUSIONS AND POLICY IMPLICATIONS

Findings from this study suggest four possible areas for policy attention:

1. Structural changes within second-level education;

2. Increasing the awareness of the effects of work in schools and among parents;

3. Issues regarding legislation and the enforcement of legislation;

4. Student financial support.

6.4.1: Structural changes within second-level education

This study has implications for two features of the educational system: firstly, school organisation and climate within second-level schools; and secondly, the degree of linkage between schools and workplaces.

This study indicates that part-time work to some extent acts as a channel out of school for young people who are disaffected with school life. School drop-out is often preceded by student engagement in a relatively heavy paid workload outside of school coupled with recurring absenteeism. The continuing gender and social class differences in patterns of early school leaving must be seen, at least to some extent, in the context of differential participation in paid work outside school. The challenge for policy is to provide a way of enriching the school experience in such a way as to discourage part-time work or at least maintain it at manageable levels.

Previous research has shown that the climate of the school has a significant effect on student retention and performance (Smyth, 1999; McCoy, 2000). It is important, therefore, that the creation of a positive school climate becomes a focus of school development planning through, for example, the development of structures designed to promote student involvement in the school. Research has also shown that the provision of subjects with a practical orientation may enhance student engagement in schoolwork (Smyth et al., 2004). Attention should be given to incorporating practical activities into second-level subjects, where possible, and to investigating more innovative forms of assessment than terminal examinations alone.

In general, the Irish educational system can be seen as "academic" in nature rather than vocationally oriented with relatively underdeveloped formal links between school and the workplace (see Smyth et al., 2001). With the exception of apprenticeships, there are currently no formal mechanisms for combining work and study in the Irish context. However, the introduction of two programmes (the Leaving Certificate Applied Programme and the Leaving Certificate Vocational Programme) has resulted in the incorporation of periods of (unpaid) work experience into upper second-level education. In addition, students taking the Transition Year programme, take part in work experience, although the length and nature of the placement varies across schools (see Smyth, Hannan, Byrne, forthcoming). The presence of formal work experience placements for a significant proportion of young people now exists side-by-side with a considerable level of informal part-time employment. The pattern of combining work and study on an informal basis has now become a common one, especially among those in senior cycle. However, no linkages have been developed between the students' experiences of paid and unpaid work. Students do not receive formal recognition for their paid employment outside school and are not encouraged to apply their school-based learning to the work context.

The challenge in policy terms is to find a way of balancing the potential negative and positive effects of part-time work by drawing upon and recognising the skills acquired by young people outside of school and developing more innovative ways of combining work and study, especially for those students at risk of dropping out of full-time education. One possibility would be the development of an accreditation system for work experience outside school. Pilot projects in Britain and Australia have looked at ways of giving recognition within the school system to the skills acquired by young people in the workplace. A more radical approach would involve changing the educational system in such a way as to facilitate young people formally combining work and study with structured linkages between the two experiences. In many European countries, young people combine work and study through an apprenticeship system within the framework of the initial education system (see, for example, the dual system in Germany). In Flanders, the compulsory school-leaving age is 18 but young people can combine part-time school attendance with part-time employment from the age of 16. It is clear that, in order to promote student retention and maximise their learning from (paid and unpaid) work, more innovative ways of combining work and study should be investigated within the Irish context.

6.4.2: Public awareness

Much of the media debate on part-time working has taken place in the absence of information on the effects of part-time work on student outcomes. Students (and their parents) have not had the information to make an informed choice about their participation in employment. An initial starting-point should be the dissemination of such information to all schools (and to all parents) on the effects of (excessive) part-time work and recommendations should be made regarding the maximum hours second-level students should work. Schools should be assisted in adopting policies to support and accommodate manageable hours of part-time work by students. Above all, school authorities should be aware of the nature and intensity of the employment in which their students engage.

The Skills Initiative Unit has suggested that school authorities should enter into agreements on guidelines with parent organisations and parents in relation to attendance, homework and term-time work and other activities. However, case-study evidence from our study indicates that school disapproval is not a strong factor in students' decision to work and school policy alone is unlikely to be an effective deterrent. Discouraging students from engaging in paid work in the first place may be more effective than asking students to give up their employment.

6.4.3: Legislation and enforcement

Evidence from the school case-studies would appear to indicate that some students are working longer hours than are permitted. This is given further weight by the fact that almost one-quarter of first year students in eleven case-study schools were found to be working outside school, more than half of them on weekday evenings. Almost all of these students were below the legal age for paid employment.[1] Enforcement of legislation is therefore a key area in the curtailment of excessive and "out-of-hours" working by students: this should involve the inclusion of employers, schools and parents in strategies to limit the employment of students. A register of all employers and second-level workers should be kept, including details of the type of job and hours/days worked. Some school principals have commented on their lack of control in the area, due to the lack of enforcement of legislation. As one principal commented:

> Unless there is a consistent policy which would be adhered to and implemented fully, it is very difficult for principals to do anything but advise. I call on the Department to have a policy on full-time students working, for example to curtail the number of hours they can work, the times they can work and the environment in which work takes place, to legislate the parameters within which work occurs because it is definitely hindering the performance of young people.

---

[1] These data derive from a study of first-year students funded by the National Council for Curriculum and Assessment (published as Smyth et al., 2004).

There is some evidence to suggest that convictions for breach of the legislation are few: in launching the Code of Practice *Concerning the Employment of Young Persons in Licensed Premises* (July 2001), the Minister commented that six employers were convicted during the period Jan 2000 to July 2001 in respect of breaches of the *Protection of Young Persons Employment Act, 1996.* It is difficult to envisage this legislation having a deterrent effect on the employment of underage youth if inspections and convictions are minimal.

6.4.4: Financial support

The provision of financial support may be seen as one way of discouraging students from dropping out of school to pursue full-time employment or from taking part-time employment while at school. One such initiative in England, the Educational Maintenance Allowance (EMA), involves a means-tested payment to 16-19-year-olds in full-time education in selected pilot areas; the initiative is be extended to a national basis from September 2004. While the initiative is still at an early stage, a positive impact on school retention and attendance has been reported (Ashworth et al., 2001). All else being equal, students who receive an EMA are less likely to have jobs than those who do not (Payne, 2001). The initiative has served more to prevent young people from taking up employment rather than bringing about their withdrawal from employment since, in many cases, the amount of the payment (£30–40) was deemed insufficient to compensate for their earnings (Legard et al., 2001).

Such a targeted approach may have some benefits for reducing social class differentiation in patterns of employment. However, it is likely that, given the level of earnings among some young people in Ireland (see Chapter 4), a support payment is unlikely to encourage young people to discontinue their employment unless the level of that payment is relatively high. In addition to the expense, a further consideration relates to the position of such a payment vis-à-vis existing financial support structures for Post-Leaving Certificate and third-level students. In particular, it is arguable whether an equivalent payment should be granted to (older) second-level students for lifestyle-related expenditure as to third-level students living away from the family home.

In conclusion, combining work and study appears to have become a relatively common pattern among second-level students in the Irish context. It is unlikely that school or parental disapproval will be enough to prevent young people from working, although there seems to be some scope for increased legislative enforcement. Part-time employment, especially that involving longer hours, appears to have a negative impact on young people's educational careers in terms of early social leaving and exam performance. On the other hand, young people feel part-time work enhances their skills and, for those who go directly into the labour market, their employment chances and pay levels are enhanced, at least in the short-term. It remains to be seen whether this initial advantage persists in the longer term. The challenge in policy terms is to find a way of making school life more attractive to students in order to minimise their involvement in paid work and, for those students who will continue to work, to find a way of facilitating a constructive combination of work and study.

REFERENCES

Ahituv, A. and Tienda, M., 2000. "Employment, Motherhood and School Continuation Decisions of Young White, Black and Hispanic Women", working/seminar paper.

Ashworth, K., Hardman, J., Liu, W.C., Maguire, S., Middleton, S., Dearden, L., Emmerson, C., Frayne, C., Goodman, A., Ichimura, H. and Meghir, C., 2001. *Education Maintenance Allowance: The First Year. A Quantitative Evaluation*, London: Department for Education and Employment.

Breen, R., Hannan, D.F. and O'Leary, R., 1995. "Returns to Education: Taking Account of Employers, Perceptions and Use of Educational Credentials", *European Sociological Review*, 11, 1: 59–74.

Canny, A., 2002. "Flexible Labour? The Growth of Student Employment in the UK", *Journal of Education and Work*, 15, 3: 277–301.

Carr, R., Wright, J. and Brody, C., 1996. "Effects of High School Work Experience a Decade Later: Evidence from the National Longitudinal Study", *Sociology of Education*, 69: 66–81.

Clancy, P., 2001. "College Entry in Focus: A Fourth National Survey of Access to Higher Education". Dublin: Higher Education Authority.

Code of Practice Concerning the Employment of Young Persons in Licensed Premises, 2001. Irish Congress of Trade Unions, Irish Hotels Federation, Licensed Vintners Association, Mandate Trade Union, National Parents Council Post-Primary, Restaurants Association of Ireland, Vintners' Federation of Ireland.

Conniffe, D., Gash, V. and O'Connell, P.J., 2000. "Evaluating State Programmes: "Natural Experiments and Propensity Scores", *Economic and Social Review*, 31 (4): 283–308.

D'Agostino, R.B., 1998. "Propensity Score Methods for Bias Reduction in the Comparison of a Treatment to a Non-randomised Control Group", *Statistics in Medicine*, 17: 2265–2281.

D'Amico, R., 1984. "Does Employment During High School Impair Academic Progress?", *Sociology of Education*, 57 (July): 152–164.

Davies, P., 1999. *Learning and Earning: The Impact of Paid Employment on Young People in Full-Time Education*, London: Further Education Development Agency.

Department of Enterprise, Trade and Employment, 1996. *Protection of Young Persons (Employment) Act, 1996*. Dublin.

Dustmann, C., Rajah, N. and van Soest, A., 1996. "Part-Time Work, School Success and School Leaving", Institute for Fiscal Studies Discussion Paper Series.

Dustmann, C., Rajah, N. and Smith, S., 1997. "Teenage Truancy, Part-Time Working and Wages", *Journal of Population Economics*, 10, 4: 425–442.

Entwisle, D.R., Alexander, K.L. and Olson, L.S., 2000. "Early Work Histories of Urban Youth", *American Sociological Review*, 65 (April): 279–297.

Fahey, T. and Russell, H., 2001. *Older People's Preferences for Employment and Retirement in Ireland*. Dublin: National Council on Ageing and Older People.

Gade, E. and Paterson, L., 1980. "A Comparison of Working and Non-Working High School Students on School Performance, Socioeconomic Status and Self-Esteem", *Vocational Guidance Quarterly*, 29: 65–69.

Gordon, A., 1980. "Leaving School: a question of money?", *Educational Studies*, 6, 1: 43–55.

Green, D.I., 1990. "High-School Student Employment in Social Context: Adolescents' Perceptions of the Role of Part-Time Work", *Adolescence*, 25: 425–434.

Greenberger, E. and Steinberg, L., 1986. *When Teenagers Work: The Psychological and Social Costs of Adolescent Employment*, New York: Basic Books.

Hannan, D.F., McCabe, B., McCoy, S., 1998. *Trading Qualifications for Jobs: Overeducation and the Irish Youth Labour Market*, Dublin: Oak Tree Press/ESRI.

Hannan, D.F., Smyth, E., McCullagh, J., O'Leary, R., McMahon, D., 1996. *Co-education and Gender Equality: Exam Performance, Stress and Personal Development*. Dublin: Oak Tree Press/ESRI.

Hotz, J.V., Xu, L., Tienda, M. and Ahituv, A., 1999. "Are There Returns to the Wages of Young Men from Working While in School?", US, June 1999.

Jordan, W.J. and Nettles, S.M., 1999. "How Students Invest Their Time Out of School: Effects on School Engagement, Perceptions of Life Chances and Achievement", Center for Research on the Education of Students Placed at Risk, Report No. 29.

Legard, R., Woodfield, K. and White, C., 2001. "Staying Away or Staying On? A Qualitative Evaluation of the Education Maintenance Allowance", London: Department for Education and Employment.

Leonard, M., 1995. "Labouring to Learn: Students' Debt and Term-time Employment in Belfast", *Higher Education Quarterly*, 49, 3: 229–247.

Light, A., 2001. "In-School Work Experience and the Returns to Schooling", *Journal of Labour Economics*, 19, 1: 65–93.

Lillydahl, J., 1990. "Academic Achievement and Part-Time Employment of High School Students", *Journal of Economic Education*, 21: 307–316.

Lucas, R., 1997. "Youth, Gender and Part-Time Work Students in the Labour Process", *Work Employment and Society*, 11, 4, Dec: 595–614.

Markel, K.S. and Frone, M.R., 1998. "Job Characteristics, Work-School Conflict and School Outcomes", *Journal of Applied Psychology*, 83, 2: 277–287.

Marsh, H., 1991. "Employment during High School: Character Building or a Subversion of Academic Goals?" *Sociology of Education*, 64: 172–189.

McCoy, D., Duffy, D. and Smyth, D. (2000). *Quarterly Economic Commentary* September 2000, Dublin: Economic and Social Research Institute.

McCoy, S. 2000. "Do Schools Count: Key School Structural and Process Influences on Early School Leaving?", The Queen's University of Belfast, Unpublished Ph.D. thesis.

McNeal, R.B., 1997. "Are Students Being Pulled Out of High School? The Effect of Adolescent Employment on Dropping Out", *Sociology of Education*, 70 (July): 206–220.

McVicar, D. and McKee, B., 2001. "Part Time Work during Post-compulsory Education and Examination Performance: Help or Hindrance?", NIERC Working Paper No. 63.

Micklewright, J., Rajah, N. and Smith, S., 1994. "Labouring and Learning: Part-Time Work and Full-Time Education", *National Institute Economic Review*, 2: 73–85.

Mizen, P., Bolton, A. and Pole, C., 1999. "School Age Workers: The Paid Employment of Children in Britain", *Work, Employment and Society*, 13, 3: 423–438.

Morgan, M., 2000. "School and Part-Time Work in Dublin — The Facts", Dublin Employment Pact, Policy Paper No. 4.

Oettinger, G.S., 1999. "Does High School Employment Affect High School Academic Performance?", *Industrial and Labor Relations Review*, 53, 1: 136–151.

Pabilonia, S.W., 1999 "The Role of the Family in Determining Youth Employment", University of Washington, November 1999.

Payne, J., 2001. "Post-16 Students and Part-time Jobs: Patterns and Effects", London: Department for Education and Employment.

Post, D. and Pong, S.L., 2000. "Employment During Middle School: The Effects on Academic Achievement in the U.S. and Abroad", *Educational Evaluation and Policy Analysis,* 22, 3: 273–298.

Robinson, L., 1999. *The Effects of Part-time Work on School Students*, Victoria: Australian Council for Educational Research.

Ruhm, Christopher J., 1995. "The Extent and Consequences of High School Employment", *Journal of Labour Research*, 16, 3, Summer: 293–303.

Ruhm, C.J., 1997. "Is High School Employment Consumption or Investment", *Journal of Labour Economics*, 15, 4: 735–776.

Ruscoe, G., Morgan, J.C. and Peebles, C., 1996. "Students Who Work", *Adolescence*, 31, 123, Fall: 625–632.

Schill, W.J., McCartin, R. and Meyer, K., 1985. "Youth Employment: Its Relationship to Academic and Family Variables", *Journal of Vocational Behaviour*, 26: 155–163.

Schoenhals, M., Tienda, M. and Schneider, B., 1998. "The Education and Personal Consequences of Adolescent Employment", *Social Forces*, 77 (2): 723–761.

Sexton, J.J., 2002. "Recent Developments in the Economy and Labour Market" in *Quarterly Economic Commentary*, Dublin: ESRI.

Skills Initiative Unit, 2002. "Student Under Achievement and Part-Time Work", Discussion document.

Singh, K., 1998. "Part-time Employment in High School", *Journal of Educational Research*, 91, 3: 131–139.

Smyth, E., 1999. "Educational Inequalities among school leavers in Ireland 1979–1994", *The Economic and Social Review*, 30, 3: 267–284.

Smyth, E. and Hannan, D.F., 2000. "Education and Inequality" in B.Nolan, P.J. O'Connell and C.T. Whelan (eds.), *Bust to Boom? The Irish Experience of Growth and Inequality*, Dublin: IPA.

Smyth, E., Hannan, C. and Byrne, D. (forthcoming). *The Transition Year Programme: An Assessment*, Dublin: The Liffey Press/ESRI.

Smyth, E., Gangl, M., Raffe, D. et al, 2001. "A Comparative Analysis of Transitions from Education to Work in Europe (CATEWE): Final Report", Report to the European Commission.

Smyth, E., McCoy, S. and Darmody, M., 2004. *Moving Up: The Experiences of First Year Students in Post-Primary Education*, Dublin: The Liffey Press/ESRI.

Steinberg, L. and Fegley, S. and Dornbusch, S.M., 1993. "Negative Effect of Part-Time Work on Adolescent Adjustment: Evidence from a Longitudinal Study", *Developmental Psychology*, 29: 171–180.

Stern, D. and Briggs, D., 2001. "Does Paid Employment Help or Hinder Performance in Secondary School? Insights from US High School Students", *Journal of Education and Work*, 14, 3: 355–372.